JINN SORCERY

JINN SORCERY

Rain Al-Alim

SCARLET IMPRINT MMXVIII

© Rain Al-Alim, 2018.
Published by Scarlet Imprint
Edited by Paul Holman and Peter Grey
Designed and typeset by Alkistis Dimech

ISBN 978-1-912316-15-1

All rights reserved. No part of this book may be reproduced in any form, without prior permission being obtained in writing from the publisher.

WWW.SCARLETIMPRINT.COM

Contents

Preface xi

Conjuring jinn for dream revelation 1
Al-Mandal: Techniques of scrying 5
Jinn workings and evocation rites 28
Summoning the personal qarīn 62
The seven jinn evictions 65

Bibliography 71
Index of conjurations 74

Disclaimer

The author of this book has taken care to ensure the authenticity of the information and the techniques contained herein. He is not responsible, in whole or in part, for any harm or injury, physical, mental or otherwise, which may befall the reader as a result of following the instructions in this book. It is understood that many of the techniques, rituals and conjurations are given for scholarly purposes, and that there exists a potential for injury when using the techniques or practices described. Neither the publisher nor the author guarantees the legality or the appropriateness of the techniques, acts, rituals, exercises and conjurations contained herein.

Preface

A belief in magic and the jinn plays an important part in the Arab world.[1] The Arabs believe in the existence of beings to whom they ascribe the generic name of *jinn* [الجن]; the primary meaning of the root *j-n-n* means 'to hide; to conceal.'[2] The grammatically correct masculine singular form in Arabic is *jinnī* and the feminine equivalent *jinnīya* [جني / جنية]; jinn is the plural form.

Islam accepts the existence of subtle, non-human entities as part of God's creation. According to the Qur'ān, the jinn are invisible spirits that live among us and were created before men. *The Thousand and One Nights* (*Kitāb 'alf layla wa-layla*, كِتَاب أَلْف لَيْلَة وَلَيْلَة) contains a considerable body of lore on the jinn, both those who have accepted Islam, and those who are heretics, their modes of appearance and disappearance, their enchantments, their loves and desires, and the means of capturing and binding them.

It is commonly believed that these spirits live in tribes and nations, and belong to different religions, whether Muslim, Christian, Jewish, or infidels (unbelievers). The Jewish and idolatrous jinn are

1 There are different theories concerning the origin of the jinn. The Islamic account can be found in the Qur'ān (*Sūrat ar-Raḥmān*: 15); in ancient Rome, the term *genii*, the plural form of the Latin word *genius*, referred to the spirits that watched over every man; according to *The Thousand and One Nights* numerous spirits and entities exist alongside humans and interact with each other just as they do with humans.

2 Another name for them is khāfi, which has the same meaning.

generally held to be the worst kinds, whilst the Muslim jinn are considered good and pious. The wicked *shayāṭīn* [شياطين], or devils, are the servants of Iblīs who launch harmful attacks against humans. The spirits are organised in tribes under chiefs and princes. Each jinnī is dangerous because, like the Arabs, the power of his tribe is behind him and will avenge him if need be.

Jinn are characterised by their transient, volatile forms, and can change their physical appearance as they desire. Whilst angels, who are created from light, are considered to be benevolent, the nature of the jinn is ambivalent. There are good and evil ones among them, but generally the evil and dangerous connotations prevail, with the shayāṭīn viewed as being particularly sinister.

In the Arab-Muslim tradition, the jinn are neither the souls of the dead, ghosts roaming the earth, nor are they forces of evil battling the forces of good. Jinn are intelligent and subtle beings, powerful creatures that can travel long distances in the twinkling of an eye. They are able to pass through walls, swim underwater, and reveal the future. But, like humans, they eat, drink, make love and die.

The jinn are as innumerable as the sand, being of different types, different sexes, different religions, different races, and speaking different languages. They may communicate through a human host or one may hear them as disembodied voices. Sometimes one may glimpse them, as they can assume the shape of humans or animals in order to appear to us.

Yet jinn are different from humans in nature, appearance and power. According to the Qur'ān, they are born of smokeless fire while human beings are created out of clay (*Sūrat ar-Raḥmān*: 14–15), which makes physical contact between them impossible. Also, jinn are invisible beings: they can see humans whilst they cannot be seen.[3] Moreover, jinn are capable of performing miracles: the Qur'ān mentions their ability to traverse time and space at incredible speeds and to transport unbelievable weights (*Sūrat al-Naml*: 39).

3 According to Qurānic lore, our world is separated from the world of the jinn by an invisible veil.

Because of their numerous powers, the jinn account for much of the magic perceived by humans, often cooperating with magicians to accomplish their feats. There is a fundamental belief in *al-ghayb* [الغيب], the unseen and the unknown, in the Islamic faith. Sorcery, or *siḥr* [سحر], is viewed as an attempt to control the forces of nature, either for good or evil purposes. As such, it is forbidden according to orthodox Islam, unless it is done with God's explicit permission, as in the case of miracles performed by those favoured by Him.

Magic and sorcery have been practised widely in Arab culture. An individual practicing sorcery is called *sāḥir* [ساحر], plural *saḥarah* [سحرة]. Siḥr is traditionally distinguished as being either natural/sympathetic or demonic. Natural magic makes use of the hidden properties (*khawāṣ* خواص) of natural substances, whilst demonic magic involves the help of spirits and jinn, usually malevolent demons (*shayāṭīn*).

Although the jinn often visit mankind of their own free will, there are also many ways by which sorcerers can summon them. These methods, if used clumsily, may expose them to temptation and peril. For most people in the Muslim world the jinn represent dangerous and demonic creatures, but sometimes they can render helpful service.

It is believed that jinn manifest in human beings through fits of possession. When the body falls to the ground in an epileptic or paralytic fit, it is said that the jinnī inside it manifests its presence. Thus, an act of exorcism is needed to evict, or at least appease, the jinnī, depending on whether the host benefits or suffers from the spirit possession. This process is accomplished through various rites.

The practice of exorcism, or jinn eviction, is called *ṣir* or *ṣara*. The term *ṣara'a* is used by Middle-Eastern healers and magicians for the healing process, or exorcising the jinnī through struggle and submission. It is derived from the Arabic word *ṣṣar'* (to throw to the ground; to have an epileptic fit). Some healers work through a jinnī *khabīr* (informant), who instructs them as to how they should treat the patient, by reading their future and so on, or revealing to them the location of a hidden spell (*siḥr*), which has to be extracted or undone.[4]

The jinn can cause many different types of sickness and harm to humans, affecting their psychology, mood, health, wealth, possessions, relationships, business, or studies. Bad dreams, fainting, and unusual diseases can indicate possession by a jinnī. Any kind of mental or physical disorder could be caused by a jinnī, particularly if modern methods of diagnosis and therapy yield no results. Therefore, mental instability and disorder are frequently attributed to a jinnī's power, and the word *majnūn* [مجنون] (crazy; possessed) is used in such cases.

CLASSIFICATIONS AND TYPES OF JINN

There exists a rich language to describe the jinn, with terminology for the different types of jinn: *ḥinn* is said to denote one tribe of weaker jinn, or those spirits intermediate between jinn and men;[5] *ghūl* [غول] comes from the root *ghala* [غل], meaning to seize; *'afārīt* [عفاريت] (singular: *'ifrīt* عفريت) are usually malevolent – the verb *'afara* [عفر], from which the noun is derived, means to roll in the dust, (i.e. to bring down), and so the name is used of powerful spirits; *mārid* [مارد] is derived from *marada* [مرد], to be rebellious – these jinn are said to be the most powerful and are very arrogant; *si'lāt* usually denotes a female spirit; the *shiqq* has the form of a bisected man (as if divided longitudinally), and often attacks lonely travellers; *'amir* is any jinnī that lives in a house or near people; and *roḥāni* is a jinnī

4 In Arabic magic, when a harmful spell is cast upon someone, it is often written and then buried in the ground or in a grave, so the way to reverse or undo the spell requires it to be found and exhumed. In this context, the jinn can be asked to reveal where exactly a buried spell is located.

5 In Islam there is not agreement as to whether the ḥinn are actually jinn or a different species. Some authors, such as Zakarīyā Ibn Muḥammad al-Qazwīnī, say that they are weaker jinn closer to animals, others that they were created before the jinn and humans.

who is said to live in the air between the earth and the sky. Furthermore, they are often alluded to by such expressions as *al-aryāḥ* (the winds/airs); *al-jawad* (the bountiful/generous); *sukkan al-'ammar* (resident jinn); as *sidna* 'our lord'; and *rjāl al-ḥafiya*, 'the hidden men.'

Jinn are ranked by their magical strength and standing within their own society, with greater jinn being highly intelligent and extremely dangerous while lesser ones are more akin to mischief-makers. The social organisation of the jinn community resembles that of a royal court, in which most of the jinn are offspring of the seven jinn kings, categorised as archdemons and leaders of the infernal hosts. These rulers are traditionally associated with the seven planets, with a colour and a day of the week attributed to each of them. They have many subjects and advisors, drawn from the tribes under their rulership. The old Arabic grimoires refer to them as the seven terrestrial kings (*mulūk al-arḍīya*). They are governed in turn by the seven angels of the days.

In addition, Arabic occult lore gives a number of different leaders, kings and queens of the jinn, for example King Taresh is the ruler of the *'ummar al-buyūt* (dwellers in houses), all jinn who reside with humans.

The *qarīn* is another important type of jinnī. Qarīn (pl. *quranā'*) or *hamzād* means 'constant companion,' and is derived from the root *q-r-n*, meaning to join, to couple, or to yoke. It is believed that for each person in the human realm there exists a qarīn in the parallel jinn realm. Quranā' may be female or male: qarīn is قرين (masculine) and qarīna قرينة (feminine). Usually a qarīn resides in a male and a qarīna in a female. Sometimes they are described as our individual shayṭān and most of them are believed to be evil, they try to lead us astray throughout our lives. Abba Deebaj is the king of all quranā'.

It is the qarīn who knows the character and deeds of the dead. During seances a jinnī can pretend to contact the dead allowing them to speak to the living, when in fact the jinnī has contacted the qarīn of the dead person. The qarīn, as the constant companion of the dead person knows his entire life history, can mimic his voice and accurately answer any questions, thus fooling those present.

Iblīs or Shayṭān is the Islamic equivalent of the Devil. He is the ruler of all underworld and malevolent jinn or shayāṭīn. Iblīs is viewed as a demonic figure, or fallen jinnī, whose primary task is to incite humans to commit evil through deception. Shayṭān and his minions are 'whisperers,' in that they whisper into the hearts of both humans and jinn, urging them to sin.

Iblīs most likely is a contraction of the Greek *diabolos*, although the Arab philologists derive the name from the root *b-l-s*, 'because Iblīs has nothing to expect (*ublisa*) from the mercy of God.'[6] He is also known as 'adūww Allāh (the enemy of God) and al-'Adūww (the Enemy). According to a hadith narrated by Ibn 'Abbas, Iblīs revealed that his name had been 'Azāzīl, and according to another account that it had been Al-Ḥārith.

WAYS OF SUMMONING THE JINN

Arabic magic assimilated many magical procedures from different cultures such as those of Mesopotamia, Greece, Egypt, Chaldea and India. Sorcery by the means of jinn plays a significant role in the Middle-Eastern magical tradition. Most Islamic occult manuals contain a variety of spells for summoning jinn, whether for acquiring hidden knowledge, for accomplishing various deeds, or employing them in the search for treasure. These are commonly viewed as illicit forms of magic because they are addressed not solely to God, but to jinn and demons. Many of the methods and techniques covered in the old Arabic manuscripts and grimoires are unknown to Western readers. This book is primarily intended for this audience, presenting a complete translation of jinn summoning techniques selected from multiple magical treatises that will bridge the gap between the Western and Islamic occult sciences. My wish is to facil-

6 Wensinck, A. J. and Gardet, L., 'Iblīs,' in: Encyclopaedia of Islam, second edition, edited by P. Bearman, Th. Bianquis, C. E. Bosworth, E. van Donzel, W. P. Heinrichs.

itate the exchange of esoteric ideas between the two worlds, and to inspire further research on the subject. But first, some introductory remarks are needed concerning the different methods of conjuring jinn among the Arab magicians.

AL-MANDAL

The practice of gazing at smooth surfaces or into clear depths to produce visions is universal. The art of scrying, as cultivated in Muslim lands, is called *darb al-mandal*, drawing the circle, or *istinzāl arwah*, to draw down the spirits. The term 'mandal' would seem to be a general one for magical ceremonies.The magician begins by drawing a circle on the ground, within which he sits while invoking the demons. This practice, also known as *fath al-mandal*, the opening of mandal, is a specialised ritual or divination that seeks the aid of the jinn. Although these practices were deemed applicable to many situations, such as providing information about past and present events, finding lost objects, getting news about an absent person or finding buried treasure, they were predominantly employed for the diagnosis of possession and to identify thieves.

The Hebrew equivalent of this practice is called *sarei shemen*, 'the princes of the oil,' first mentioned in the Talmud as a divinatory technique employed by the Jews. They had learned this from the Babylonians during the captivity. The Babylonian practice of oil magic is recorded as far back as 2000 BCE, and their use of oil in divination, as well as in other kinds of magic, came in turn from the Sumerians. In all these techniques the diviner instructed a naive subject, usually a child, to focus his gaze on a smooth, bright surface, where the princes, most commonly conceived of as demons, were expected to appear. Thus, an appropriate locus might be produced by anointing the fingernail with oil (the princes of the oil), by pouring a drop of oil on the palm (the princes of the hand), into a vessel full of water, or by anointing the edges of an empty glass.

The Arabs believe that the mandal is accomplished with the aid of the jinn. The idea is to establish contact with the jinn at a safe distance by using a surrogate scryer, traditionally a prepubescent boy. Oil mixed with black ink was poured into his hand to create the scrying surface. This was followed with magical incantations to put the seer into a hypnotic trance. The magician asked questions and the child staring into the oil provided the answers. A single figure usually appeared, then a large company, and finally their chief (ra'is, malik, sulṭān), of whom the questions would be asked, or a further vision sought.

There are many different types of mandal rite. Almost every Arabic book of magic mentions such techniques, along with the *mulūk ar-ruhaniya*, the spiritual kings, and the *a'wan ulwiya* or *as-sufliya*, the celestial and infernal helpers who appear during the ritual to carry out the magician's will. In most texts, the summoned jinn are asked to participate in a feast, the details of which are specified. All this is done to solicit their cooperation by creating a benign and auspicious setting.

DREAM DIVINATION TECHNIQUES

In antiquity people shared the view that a dream can be, and in many instances is, a meaningful message sent to a person from the gods. The unique quality of the information delivered in dreams and the desire to gain access to it generated initiatic practices for accessing such dreams or, more accurately, those who send them. Magical practices for dream revelation – that is, the application of ritual methods of adjuration and gestures to subdue a heavenly being into appearing in a dream and revealing any desired or concealed matter to the dreamer – were employed in the Greco-Roman world. Examples of these techniques are recorded in the Greek Magical Papyri.[7]

There are two branches of the practice of dream revelation. One strove for information through dreamed signs interpreted in terms

7 PGM VII/359–369, 478–490, 703–726, XXIIb/27–35.

of Holy Scripture. The other aspired for a clear, explicit message from the mouth of a dreamed entity. The difference between them lay in the figure of the mediator between the heavenly message and man. In the first case the heavenly message was sent directly into the dream, in a coded form. No heavenly mediator was involved, but subsequently a human interpreter was needed, whether the dreamer or someone else, in order to interpret the message. Conversely, no human intervention was required in the second case, since the message was delivered explicitly and clearly from the mouth of the heavenly mediator who appeared in the dream.

In Islam, there is a parallel concept called *istikhāra* (dream incubation), an Arabic term for praying to God for guidance in making an important decision. Istikhāra is still widely practiced, particularly by the Sufis, a mystical sect of Islam. The goal of istikhāra is to seek divine guidance on whether to perform an action in waking life, and it is seen as licit magic performed with God's help. Here the diviner constructs an Islamic amulet or simply writes a passage from the Qur'ān on a piece of paper, and prays to Allāh for the solution to the problem before going to sleep with his head resting on the talisman. The answer is revealed in the diviner's dreams.

Dreams can be used in conjunction with a wide variety of techniques, including those which are not classified as Islamic. This form of istikhāra is seen as a forbidden or illicit practice because the person is seeking the aid of a jinnī who reveals the sought after information. Seeking the intercession of a jinnī to discover one's calling in life was pre-Islamic, incubated in classical antiquity, and has survived in spite of Muslim orthodoxy, which absolutely rejected it.

SUMMONING THROUGH DIRECT ENCOUNTER

The invocation of jinn has been considered as incompatible with Islam, since it is necessary to call other names than that of God during the summoning. The people who carry out the incantations bear the title *mu'azzimun* (enchanters, sorcerers) and see no contradiction with Islam in their actions, most of them being religious figures and spiritual healers. The use of magical practices and spells, or *aza'im*, is believed to be derived from *al-a'zm*, meaning steadfastness/resolve. The root of *'azama* means to decide, to invite or to enchant. When the exorcist or the sorcerer says *'azamtu 'alayka* ('I order you' or 'I conjure you') to a jinnī, he compels it to obey.

Usually the magician (*as-saḥir*) has power over the jinn and the other spirits (*arwah*) because he has made a pact with them. The jinn become servants of the sorcerer and help him in the practice of his work and magic. The jinnī that is employed in this manner is called a *khādim* (servant), though the term may also be used of an angel or a demon. In Islamic occultism *khādim* refers to a spiritual servant, who has to be invoked by magic.

The complex rites of jinn subordination are described in the Arabic magical treatises, and the different jinn have different powers. They can levitate their owner, make them invisible, bring them news or treasures, or confer upon them the power to influence people. These books and manuals of magic are mostly printed in Egypt, Lebanon and Algeria, but professional magicians prefer to rely on the use of manuscripts, considering the printed books to be inferior. It is believed that spells will be more successful if taken from manuscripts which the sorcerer has inherited, usually from his ancestors.

One can learn the methods of conjuring in two ways, either through the study of magical literature, or under the direct guidance of a magician who already has experience with the jinn. The jinn can also take their own initiative to contact a person, but we have to make contact with them by performing rites or invocations. It is generally considered that the jinn must answer an invocation, but it is not an absolute rule.

Contact with the jinn is usually associated with selfish goals. The lust for occult knowledge, or the prospect of money and material riches, can awaken the desire to seek contact with the jinn. But they can also be used beneficially in healings and exorcisms.

The magical rite of conjuring jinn through a direct encounter is called *tahdīr al-jinn* (attracting the jinn), *taskhīr al-jinn* (coercing jinn into forced labour), or *khidmat/istikhdam* (employment/utilisation of the jinn), and it is usually a complicated ceremony with a set of specific requirements and observations that must be met.

It is prescribed that the operator must be in a state of purity. He must perform a ritual ablution (*wuḍū'*), engage in fasting, and abstain from meat or animal products for a given period of time. The location of the operation is to be an isolated and a secret place, as is indicated in the magical texts by the term *khalwā* (seclusion). The exact times of the operation are often carefully calculated according to the lunar cycle, astrological influences, planetary hours and days.

Except for the prayers and Qur'ānic surāts that should be recited, most of the magical incantations are incomprehensible and contain foreign and barbarous names (*nomina barbara*) or the so called Suryani names, *asma' Suryaniah*. Suryani or Proto-Syriac[8] is considered to be a magical language which is spoken in the Celestial Spheres and used by the old prophets. Most of the conjurations and the jinn names are derived from it.

No serious ceremony of jinn invocation can occur without the burning of certain incenses from the Muslim magical pharmacopoeia, of which the most common are (benzoin), *louban* (frankincense), *oud* (aloeswood), *misk* (musk), *kuzbara* (cilantro), *bakhoor al-Sudan* (gum elemi),[9] and *mastaki* (gum mastic), along with other perfumes of vegetable or animal origin. After a period of intense recitation of the incantations and extensive burning of incense, the jinnī will appear in the smoke. The sorcerer should remain strong and without fear. Requests or orders can now be delivered to the summoned

8 Suryani may be related to Syriac or Aramaic, although to this day there has been no academic research into its exact origin. It may be a branch of Akkadian, the dominant language of Babylonia, or ancient Syriac.

9 Bakhoor al-Sudan is a resin used for suffumigation. I prefer to use the Arabic name because there are differing opinions as to what it is. Some Western authors say it is gum elemi (as indicated here), although some Arabic magicians identify it as black benzoin or an incense mixture with different ingredients. I am not absolutely sure, but I personally favour black benzoin, since this is what I was told in Morocco.

being. When the jinnī arrives, it is necessary to make a contract (*a'ahd*) with it. This can also refer to a personal seal or name that the jinnī will grant in exchange for certain conditions being met. At the conclusion of the operation a license to depart is given and the jinnī is sent away in peace.

I

CONJURING JINN FOR DREAM REVELATION

SEEKING GUIDANCE

Before going to sleep say: *Zaj, Bishahat, Mashhat, Shahiyat.* Recite the names one hundred times, thereafter say: *Answer, O Maymūn, by the right of these names, and show me so-and-so in my dream.*

He will come to you with the correct information, on the condition that you sleep alone.

IF YOU WANT TO SEE SOMETHING IN YOUR DREAM

Write this talisman after the sunset prayer, before going to sleep, and do not speak with anybody afterwards. Then say: *O servants of these names, show me such-and-such in my dream. If it is good show me in white or green, and if it is bad show me in black or brown.*

Afterwards put the talisman under your pillow and you will see the thing.

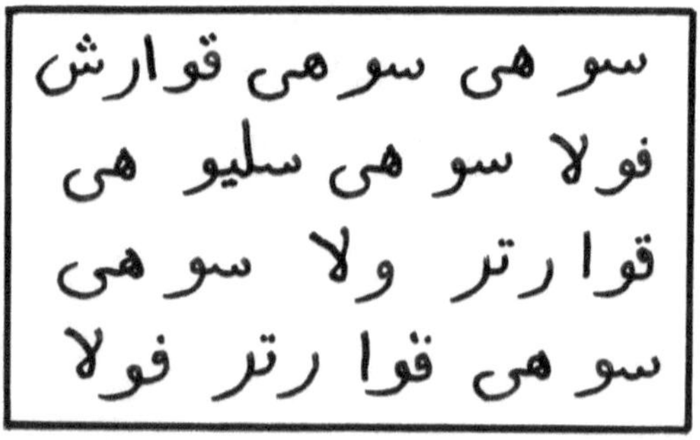

TO SEE WHATEVER YOU WISH IN A DREAM

Be in your house, whether you are using the ritual to reveal the condition of a patient, information about a theft, or something else. Inscribe *Sūrat al-Qadr* on your left hand with your right, along with the following talisman, and recite the names *An-Nur, Al-Hadi, Al-Hayy* (the Light, the Guide, the Living) and go to sleep in purity. Copy the talisman on paper, put it under your pillow, and fall asleep. The servants will inform you of whatever you wish, such as the location of buried money, or stolen goods, or if an absent person is sick or healthy, alive or dead, and whether he will come back soon.[1]

This is the talisman:

طيكل	قسورة	كمطم	مازر
مازر	طيكل	قسورة	كمطم
كمطم	مازر	طيكل	قسورة
قسورة	كمطم	مازر	طيكل

Sūrat al-Qadr · The Night of Power

إنا أنزلناه في ليلة القدر
وما أدراك ما ليلة القدر
ليلة القدر خير من ألف شهر
تنزل الملائكة والروح فيها بإذن ربهم من كل أمر
سلام هي حتى مطلع الفجر

Lo! We revealed it on the Night of Power. Ah, what will convey unto thee what the Night of Power is! The Night of Power is better than a thousand months. The angels and the Spirit descend therein, by the permission of their Lord, with all decrees. (That night is) Peace until the rising of the dawn.

1 In most Arabic magical rituals, the performer relies on the help of khadam, or servants, the beings (jinn, angels, etc.) who are connected to a talisman or summoned through a spell to accomplish the desired outcome. In this case, they are not mentioned, although the given talisman (magical square) contains the names of the four Jinn Elders: Māzer [مازر], Kamṭam [كمطم], Qaswarah [قسورة] and Ṭaykal [طيكل].

FOR DREAM REVELATION BY THE JINNĪ KHARBAṬ

This is for buried goods, or treasure, or for anything you wish to be informed of. Recite the conjuration nine times. He will come to you between wakefulness and sleep, and will inform you of whatever you wish.

This is the conjuration:

ʾAyil, ʾAyil, Hayūl, Hayul, Baqsh Shaqāsh, Baqsh Shaqāsh, Malūd, Malūd, Yāh, Yāh, Yahūh, Yahūh, Halak, Halak, Makar, Makar, Kārsh, Kārsh. Answer, O Kharbaṭ, and do so-and-so!

2

AL-MANDAL : TECHNIQUES OF SCRYING

MANDAL OF ABBA DEEBAJ

There is none other like it and it is proven and true. This will show the scryer the answer if you want to ask about a theft and the identity and location of the thief; or whether a woman is pregnant or not, and whether the foetus is a boy or a girl; or whether an absent person is alive or dead, and whether he will come back (or not); or whether a trader will profit (or not); or, in regard to belligerent people, which of them will be the victor, or whether they will be reconciled (or not), or whether some of them will die (or not); or, if there are buried goods in a place, whether they are treasure (or not), and whether the hoard is of gold, silver, copper, minerals, or something else, and whether it is cursed (or not), and how to expel its guardian, and what offering should be made for the servants, and on which day to perform the deed; or, in regard to the science of *kīmiyā'*,[1] whether you will obtain harm or benefit from its working, and whether it will produce profit; or, in regard to the science of *sīmiyā'*,[2] whether it is true or false, and whether its performer will receive a firm answer (or not); or about the magic laid on any place (if you bring an enchanted person and want to neutralise the magic placed upon him, feed him with the Verses of Breaking Magic in cold food,[3] and Allah be glorified, for He knows best);[4] or about a missing person, a fugitive, a runaway, a rival, about livestock and building and planting and other things you want to know.

If you want to perform the operation, write the seal of Abba Deebaj that follows on the fingernail of a prepubescent boy or on his palm and blacken it with black ink and pour pure olive oil over it, and suffumigate it with frankincense and gum benzoin. Read the

1 Alchemy.

2 Letter magic.

3 The original text does not contain these verses.

4 In this bracketed section, the author inserts and explains another operation in brief, as an addition to the mandal of Abba Deebaj: If you use the rite to reveal hidden malicious magic, this will enable you to neutralise it. The instruction is given this way in between the lines in the original, so I have no other option but to translate it and present it as given.

conjuration seven times, and the boy should gaze at the oil in his palm all the while. When you complete the seventh recital say:

> *Biālfarqash, Biālfarqash, Qarqash, Qarqash, Y'amūsh, Y'amūsh. See, O little one, by the right of Shamkhālūsh, Shamkhālūsh.*
>
> *Now We have removed from thee thy covering, and piercing is thy sight this day.*[5] *Allah is the Light of the heavens and the earth. The similitude of His light is as a niche wherein is a lamp. The lamp is in a glass. The glass is as it were a shining star. (This lamp is) kindled from a blessed tree, an olive neither of the East nor of the West, whose oil would almost glow forth (of itself) though no fire touched it. Light upon light. Allah guideth unto His light whom He will. And Allah speaketh to mankind in allegories, for Allah is Knower of all things.*[6]

بالفرقش بالفرقش قرقش قرقش يعموش يعموش انظر أيها الصغير بحق شمخلوش
شمخلوش فكشفنا عنك غطاءك فبصرك اليوم حديد الله نور السماوات والأرض مثل
نوره كمشكاة فيها مصباح المصباح في زجاجة الزجاجة كأنها كوكب دري يوقد من
شجرة مباركة زيتونة لا شرقية ولا غربية يكاد زيتها يضيء ولو لم تمسسه نار نور على نور
يهدي الله لنوره من يشاء ويضرب الله الأمثال للناس والله بكل شيء عليم

These are the Verses of Revelation that you write on the boy's forehead, or on a paper placed on his forehead, and visions will be revealed upon his hands, in response to what is asked.[7] Or write the names upon him with separated letters.[8]

5 Sūrat Qaf: 22.
6 Sūrat an-Nūr: 35.
7 The vision will be revealed upon the boy's fingernails or palm.
8 In Arabic magic, to write a magical text or a Qurānic verse with separated letters means not to write them as cursive script (as is normal) but with single letters, not joined to each other.

This is the seal:

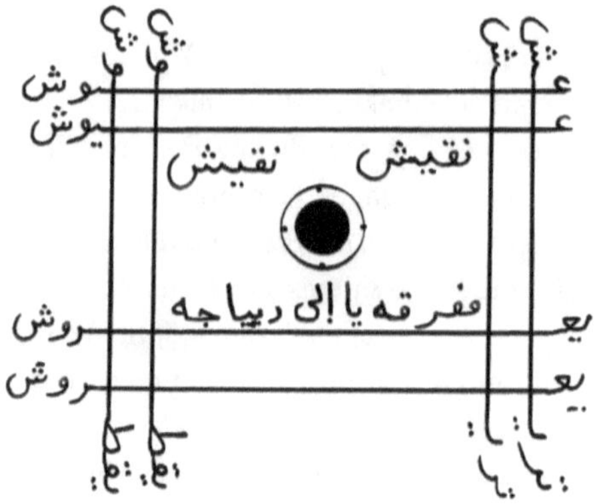

And this is the conjuration that you say:

Y'auush, Y'auush, Yamūsh, Yamūsh, Y'arūsh, Y'arūsh, Yafṭash, Yafṭash, Tarīsh, Tarīsh, Haīsh, Haīsh.

O our people! respond to Allah's summoner and believe in Him. He will forgive you some of your sins and guard you from a painful doom. And whoso respondeth not to Allah's summoner he can nowise escape in the earth, and ye (can find) no protecting friends instead of Him. Such are in error manifest.[9]

Answer, O Abba Deebaj, by the right these names have over you and the obedience you owe them, and by the right with which He said unto (heaven) and unto the earth: Come both of you, willingly or loth. They said: We come, obedient.[10]

Hasten with the answer and appear to this seer so that he sees you with his eyes and addresses you with his tongue, and show him what I ask of him without allurement or deception, and with no delay. Now! Quickly! Immediately!

9 Sūrat al-Aḥqāf: 31–32.
10 Sūrat Fuṣṣilat: 11.

PROVEN MANDAL

By this you can bring any king that you want without delay and ask him for anything, for any aid, or for any servant, or for any matter you want. Write the conjuration on your left palm with your right hand and put your right palm over the left on which is the writing. The king you call will attend to you. The incense is Indian *maskhāṭar,*[11] Ethiopian *ṭaqsh,*[12] ambergris and musk. Blend it with rosewater and aloes.

This is the conjuration that you write and recite:

بميغفكوش بميغفكوش كلا كلا كليعغش كليعغش لطش لطش فرعوش فرعوش إحضر
أيها الملك فلان أسرع من طرفة عين

Bimayghafkūsh, Bimayghafkūsh, Kalā, Kalā, Kāli'aghash, Kali'aghash, Laṭash, Laṭash, Far'aush, Far'aush, come, O King so-and-so, faster than the blink of an eye!

Preserve this conjuration and be aware of its power and of God, for it is a mystery known by the few. Guard it with great diligence.

11 In a few cases some of the names of the plants or the ingredients that are listed in the Arabic grimoires are quite obscure (even to versed Islamic magicians I know), so it is almost impossible to work out what they are exactly, especially if the author has used rural names of plants or their synonyms that are virtually unknown to Western scholars. In this case, I suspect that maskhāṭar [المسخاطر] (I am not even sure of the correct spelling since I have not found it in any dictionary) is some kind of a mixture of different compounds, rather than a single ingredient, with an Indian origin (as stated).

12 Ṭaqsh [الطقش] is a Moroccan name for certain unknown resins, or hand-made incense mixtures that are used in magical operations to repel evil forces and to attract or subjugate spirits/jinn. I have a few different ṭaqsh, which I obtained in Morocco, in my personal collection of incenses, but don't know what exactly they are and never been able to discover the information in any scholarly study or dictionary. In this particular text the ṭaqsh is described as Ethiopian, so it may be something entirely different.

MANDAL OF THE SEVEN WAYS

This may be used in seven proven ways, by means of an adult with opened sight, a small child, a cup, water, a mirror, sand, or a bottle. When the seer sees the kings, command the servants to sweep and tidy up the area for them, up to the last one that you know.[13] Thereafter you may ask about whatever you wish, such as buried goods, treasure, magic, work, an absent person, a traveller, a fugitive, or a theft. With it you can summon the king of the quranā', bring about reconciliation with the quranā', or ask about pregnancy, the foetus, or any question you wish. If you are taught how to perform the conjurations of this mandal, you will be delighted and astonished by this wonder, but keep the operation hidden and do with it what you know:[14] Allah is the Guide.

If you want to work with it, write the talisman on the palm or on the mirror, or in the other ways that were mentioned. Attach the Verses of Revelation to the forehead of the seer and recite the conjuration seven times. When all of the seven kings appear, protect the frightened seer from the horrors. He will inform you of what you wish in full. Allah is the Arbiter of Success.

This is the talisman that should be written on the palm:

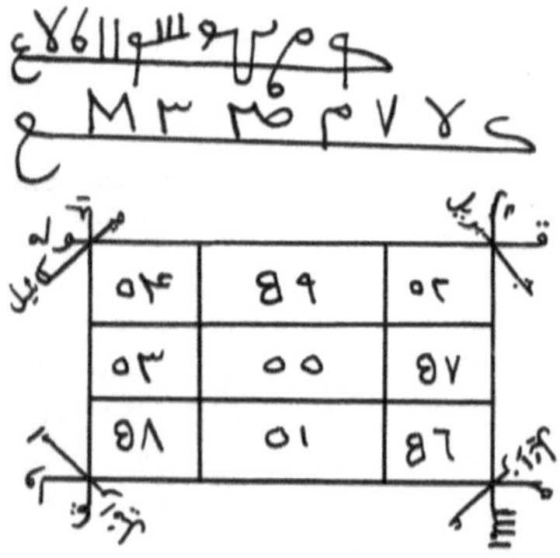

13 The servants are those of the kings, who appear before them to sweep and tidy up the area, so that it will be clean for the arrival of their rulers.

14 This means to proceed with it in the way described (as *modus operandi*).

And this is the conjuration:

I conjure you, O ye spiritual creatures obedient to Allah lord of the Creation, by the right with which he created you in stages[15] *and made your hands burning flames of fire, and by the right of Hatur, Hatur, Hathur, Hathur, Yatmur, Yatmur, Kaymūsh, Kaymush, Anuāsh, Anuāsh, Anauīl, Anauīl, Manuīl, Manuīl, Alaikūsh, Alaikūsh, Mailāhūsh, Mailāhūsh, Qudūs, Qudūs, Ahiā, Ahiā, Sharā-hiā, Sharāhiā, Adonai, Adonai, Aṣbaot, El, Shadai, Aṣbaot, El, Shadai.*

He is the Knower of the invisible and the visible, the Great, the High Exalted.[16] *The Ever-Living, the Sustainer of all existence, Who is not heedless and does not sleep, Who answers the prayer of the supplicant when he calls Him and does not disappoint a servant but gives him what he asks for. Aqsh, Aqsh, Haishā, Haishā, Maṭlishā, Maṭlishā, Tarhaqūsh, Tarhaqūsh, 'Askar, 'Askar, 'Asakar, 'Asakar, 'Akshar, 'Akshar, 'Akshīr, 'Akshīr, Qūsh, Qūsh, Ṭūsh, Ṭūsh.*

Allah hath decreed: Lo! I verily shall conquer, I and My messengers. Lo! Allah is Strong, Almighty.[17] *And every soul cometh, along with it a driver and a witness.*[18]

Answer, O terrestrial kings and sultans, and tear the veil between you and this seer so that he sees you with his eyes and addresses you with his tongue, and inform him of what I ask you. Now! Quickly! Immediately!

And lo! that verily is a tremendous oath, if ye but knew.[19]

These are the Verses of Revelation that you must write:

بالقرقش فكشفنا عنك غطاءك فبصرك اليوم حديد
وكذلك نري إبراهيم ملكوت السماوات والأرض وليكون من الموقنين

Biālqarqash. Now We have removed from thee thy covering, and piercing

15 He created you by (divers) stages. (Sūrat Nūḥ: 14).
16 Sūrat ar-Ra'd: 9.
17 Sūrat al-Mujādilah: 21.
18 Sūrat Qaf: 21.
19 Sūrat al-Wāqi'h: 76.

is thy sight this day.[20] *Thus did We show Abraham the kingdom of the heavens and the earth that he might be of those possessing certainty.*[21]

Preserve it well. It is truly proven.

PROVEN MANDAL

Employ a prepubescent boy who is born under an Air sign. Write the seal on his palm and the Verses of Revelation on his forehead and pour black ink and olive oil into the centre of his palm. Recite the conjuration seventy-one times, and burn incense: a mixture of gum sandarac, benzoin and frankincense, and ask for whatever you wish. Indeed you will witness a miracle.

This is the conjuration:

Darbaj, Darbaj, Darīj, Darīj, Bāhiāsh, Bāhiāsh, Ahiāsh, Ahiāsh, Ashmakh, Ashmakh, Shamākh, Shamākh, the Exalted above all that is blessed, the Most Exalted in the elevation of His highness. Answer, O Abba Hamid, and you, O Abba Muhammad the Diver, and you, O Abba Abdullah Al-Madhab, and, O Abba Abdul Rahman, show yourselves to this seer so that he sees you with his eyes and addresses you with his tongue by the right of the verse:

And when his Lord revealed (His) glory to the mountain He sent it crashing down. And Moses fell down senseless. And when he woke he said: Glory unto Thee! I turn unto Thee repentant, and I am the first of (true) believers,[22] *and by the right of Ahiā, Sharāhiā, Adonai, Aṣbaot, El, Shadai. And lo! that verily is a tremendous oath, if ye but knew.*[23] *Now! Quickly! Immediately!*

These are the Verses of Revelation:

20 Sūrat Qaf: 22.
21 Sūrat al-An'ām: 75.
22 Sūrat al-A'rāf: 143.
23 Sūrat al-Wāqi'ah: 76.

فكشفنا عنك غطاءك فبصرك اليوم حديد
وكذلك نري إبراهيم ملكوت السماوات والأرض وليكون من الموقنين
الله نور السماوات والأرض مثل نوره كمشكاة فيها مصباح المصباح في زجاجة الزجاجة
كأنها كوكب دري يوقد من شجرة مباركة زيتونة لا شرقية ولا غربية يكاد زيتها يضيء
ولو لم تمسسه نار نور على نور يهدي الله لنوره من يشاء ويضرب الله الأمثال للناس
والله بكل شيء عليم اكشف لناظرى الوحا

Now We have removed from thee thy covering, and piercing is thy sight this day.[24] *Thus did We show Abraham the kingdom of the heavens and the earth that he might be of those possessing certainty.*[25] *Allah is the Light of the heavens and the earth. The similitude of His light is as a niche wherein is a lamp. The lamp is in a glass. The glass is as it were a shining star. (This lamp is) kindled from a blessed tree, an olive neither of the East nor of the West, whose oil would almost glow forth (of itself) though no fire touched it. Light upon light. Allah guideth unto His light whom He will. And Allah speaketh to mankind in allegories, for Allah is Knower of all things.*[26] *Reveal to the seer. Hurry!*

This is the seal:

24 Sūrat Qaf: 22.
25 Sūrat al-An'ām: 75.
26 Sūrat an-Nūr: 35.

PROVEN MANDAL

Write the following seal in the palm or in a cup and put the Verses of Revelation on the forehead of the seer and recite the conjuration until the seer says that he sees so-and-so and then ask him whatever you wish.

This is the seal:

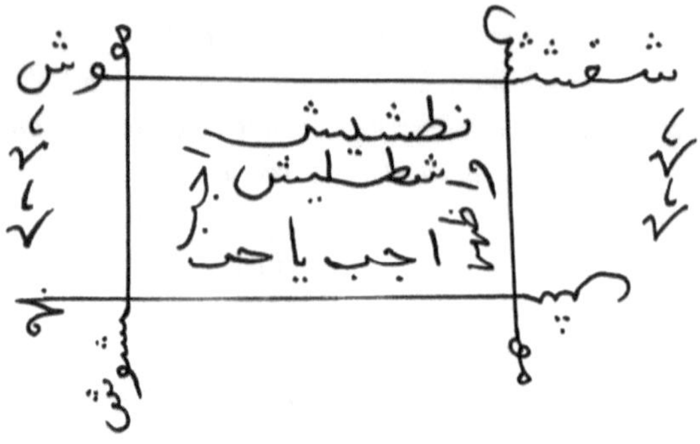

These are the Verses of Revelation:

شمشهش شمشهش معش معش هش هش نحش نحش مهش مهش شطش شطش هيا
اكشفوا الحجاب لناظوري حتي يراكم بعينه ويخاطبكم بلسانه الوحا العجل الساعة

Shamshahash, Shamshahash, Mʿash, Mʿash, Hash, Hash, Naḥash, Naḥash, Mahash, Mahash, Shaṭash, Shaṭash, come, remove the veil from the seer so that he sees you with his eyes and addresses you with his tongue. Now! Quickly! Immediately!

This is the conjuration:

Sh'ash'aush, Sh'ash'aush, M'ashush, M'ashush, Lahash, Lahash, Mahush, Mahush, Kashtalish, Kashtalish, come, descend in the form in which Allah created you. And such of them as deviated from Our command, them We caused to taste the punishment of flaming fire.[27]

27 Sūrat Saba': 12.

Hurry! Hurry! Show yourselves to the seer so that he sees you with his eyes and addresses you with his tongue, and inform him of what I ask you. Now! Quickly! Immediately!

MANDAL OF THE SEVEN KINGS

Bring the seer and pour olive oil and black ink into his palm, and incense it with coriander seeds, gum sandarac, benzoin and frankincense. Indeed the seven kings will appear and will inform the seer of what you wish. It is proven.

This is the conjuration:

'Atiun, 'Atiun, 'Afin, 'Afin, Shash, Shash, Barshul, Barshul, Aush, Aush, Huan, Huan, Batuh, Batuh, Rahuaiyl, Rahuaiyl, S'amash, S'amash, Ah, Ah, Ahiā, Sharāhiā, Ahiā, Sharāhiā, Adonai, Aṣbaot, El, Shadai. And lo! that verily is a tremendous oath, if ye but knew.[28]

Write this seal on the palm of the seer:

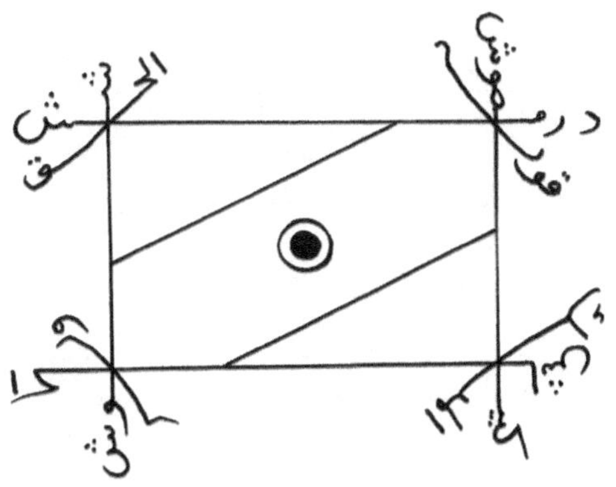

28 Sūrat al-Wāqi'ah: 76.

CELESTIAL MANDAL

Fetch a prepubescent boy and blacken his palm and pour pure olive oil over it, and suffumigate it with gum benzoin and frankincense, and recite the conjuration. And indeed the seven kings will appear to him. And after them will come seven elders. Ask them whatever you wish and they will reply to you about what is asked, such as theft and other things of concern to the attendants. It has a strong effect.

This is the conjuration:

> *Shaqmūsh, Dakshalikh, 'Askar, 'A'sakar. Say: He is Allah, the One! Allah, the eternally Besought of all! He begetteth not nor was begotten. And there is none comparable unto Him.*[29] *Lo! it is from Solomon, and lo! it is: In the name of Allah the Beneficent, the Merciful; Exalt not yourselves against me, but come unto me as those who surrender.*[30] *And lo! that verily is a tremendous oath, if ye but knew.*[31]

This is the seal that you have to write on the palm:

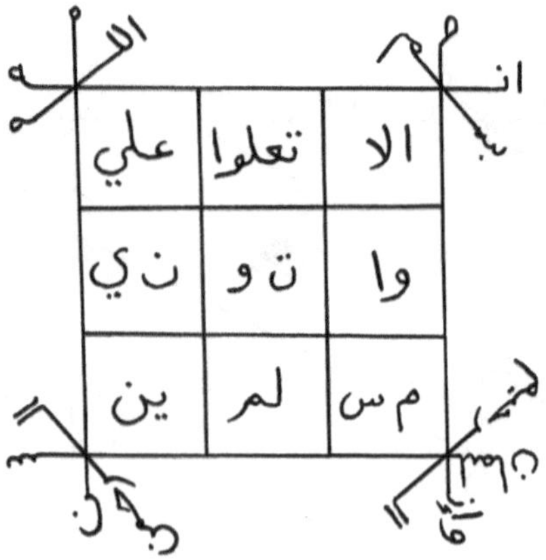

29 Sūrat al-Ikhlāṣ.
30 Sūrat an-Naml: 30–31.
31 Sūrat al-Wāqi'ah: 76

And these are the Verses of Revelation. Write them on a paper and attach it to the seer's forehead:

بالقرقش بالقرقش قرقش قرقش مخلموش مخلموش
فكشفنا عنك غطاءك فبصرك اليوم حديد
وكذلك نري إبراهيم ملكوت السماوات والأرض وليكون من الموقنين

Biālqarqash, Biālqarqash, Qarqash, Qarqash, Makhlamūsh, Makhlamūsh. Now We have removed from thee thy covering, and piercing is thy sight this day.[32] *Thus did We show Abraham the kingdom of the heavens and the earth that he might be of those possessing certainty.*[33]

PROVEN MANDAL

Perform it with a prepubescent boy using black ink and olive oil, and incense the working and recite the names, and command them to appear and give information. Indeed you will see a miracle.

This is the seal that you have to write on the seer's palm:

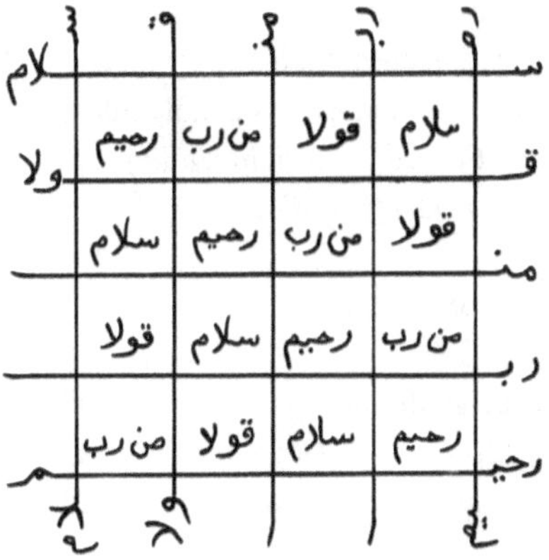

32 Sūrat Qaf: 22.
33 Sūrat al-An'ām: 75

And these are the Verses of Revelation:

فكشفنا عنك غطاءك فبصرك اليوم حديد الله نور السماوات والأرض مثل نوره كمشكاة
فيها مصباح المصباح في زجاجة الزجاجة كأنها كوكب دري يوقد من شجرة مباركة
زيتونة لا شرقية ولا غربية يكاد زيتها يضيء ولو لم تمسسه نار نور على نور يهدي الله
لنوره من يشاء ويضرب الله الأمثال للناس والله بكل شيء عليم
وكذلك نري إبراهيم ملكوت السماوات والأرض وليكون من الموقنين
قرقش قرقش قدقش قدقش قرشكش قرشكش قدشكش قدشكش بالقرقش بالقرقش
تبينوا الناظوري هذا واخرقوا الحجاب بينه وبينكم وافعلوا ما تؤمرون الوحا العجل
الساعة

Now We have removed from thee thy covering, and piercing is thy sight this day.[34] *Allah is the Light of the heavens and the earth. The similitude of His light is as a niche wherein is a lamp. The lamp is in a glass. The glass is as it were a shining star. (This lamp is) kindled from a blessed tree, an olive neither of the East nor of the West, whose oil would almost glow forth (of itself) though no fire touched it. Light upon light. Allah guideth unto His light whom He will. And Allah speaketh to mankind in allegories, for Allah is Knower of all things.*[35] *Thus did We show Abraham the kingdom of the heavens and the earth that he might be of those possessing certainty.*[36]

Qarqash, Qarqash, Qadqash, Qadqash, Qarshakash, Qarshakash, Qadshakash, Qadshakash, Biālqarqash, Biālqarqash. Reveal yourselves to this seer and tear the veil between him and you, and do what you are commanded. Now! Quickly! Immediately!

These are the names to recite:

Taighab, Taighab, Saighab, Saighab, Saighub, Saighub, Hailub, Hailub, Daghub, Daghub, Tatub, Tatub, Haj Hajij, O Shamudah, and O Abba Dhaib, hasten and tear the veil between you and this seer so that he

34 Sūrat Qaf: 22.
35 Sūrat an-Nūr: 35.
36 Sūrat al-An'ām: 75.

sees you with his eyes and addresses you with his tongue. Inform him of what I ask. Now! Quickly! Immediately! In obedience! In obedience!

The incense for the operation is Indian aloeswood, white costus, camphor and frankincense.

PROVEN MANDAL

Do not doubt it. It is revealed in the palm and in the fingernail. Blacken the palm or the fingernail or the thumbs with black ink and olive oil and recite the conjuration over it, and the boy should gaze and inform you as to what you ask. Attach the Verses of Revelation to his forehead and the talisman to his palm.

This is the talisman:

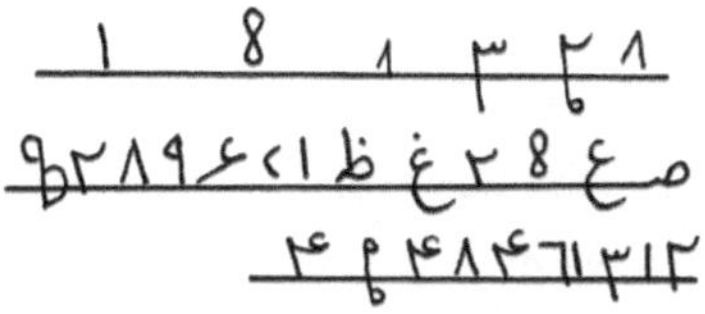

These are the figures and the Verses of Revelation:

فكشفنا عنك غطاءك فبصرك اليوم حديد

Now We have removed from thee thy covering, and piercing is thy sight this day.[37]

37 Sūrat Qaf: 22.

And this is the conjuration:

A'atūn, A'atūn, Asiūn, Asiūn, Aiusūn, Aiusūn, Jalisūn, Jalisūn, Meṭaṭron, Meṭaṭron, Qal, O Asiūn, Qal, O Asiūn, Asūm, Asūm, Alūm, Alūm, Haiūm, Haiūm.

Verily in the remembrance of Allah do hearts find rest![38] *Come and reveal yourselves to this seer so that he sees you with his eyes and addresses you with his tongue, and inform him as to what I ask of you. Now! Quickly!*

The incense is onycha, gum mastic and frankincense.

SCRYING BY YOURSELF

Take a cup made of clay and write the following conjuration on its outside. Also recite the conjuration over white salt and then trace a square around the cup with the salt.

Afterwards recite the conjuration over the cup seventy-seven times each night after the Ishā' prayer, and burn incense: a mixture of coriander seeds and white benzoin gum. Begin the operation in solitude on a Thursday. Write the seal on the bottom of the cup from underneath. The cup has to be unused and filled with well water. Gaze in the water and you will see the divine secret. Ask whatever you wish and perform the ritual with diligence and in secrecy.

This is the conjuration:

بهروش هيفا هنت هروش مروش هيلوش هيملوش ومن يزغ منهم عن أمرنا نذقه من عذاب السعير الوحا العجل الساعة

Bahrūsh, Bahrūsh, Haifā, Haifā, Hanat, Hanat, Harūsh, Marūsh, Marūsh, Haylūsh, Haymalūsh. And such of them as deviated from Our

38 Sūrat ar-Ra'd: 28.

command, them We caused to taste the punishment of flaming fire.[39]
Now! Quickly! Immediately!

And this is the talisman:

SCRYING BY YOURSELF

Write the following seal on the back of a new mirror, then recite the conjuration seventy-one times while gazing into the glass. When you finish the recitation you will see a vision in the mirror of an uncovered treasure, a treasure trove above the ground, the demand at the door, the need before you, and the aim accomplished. This is a great secret. During the recitation burn an incense of Syrian rue seeds, fresh or dry mint leaves and sarghina.[40] You can write and recite the conjuration at any time.

39 Sūrat Saba': 12.
40 Sarghina, Saghine or Sarghand, also sometimes Sumbul, (*Corrigiola telephii-folia*), is a small dried root from Morocco used as an incense. It is very popular in the herbal shops there.

This is the seal:

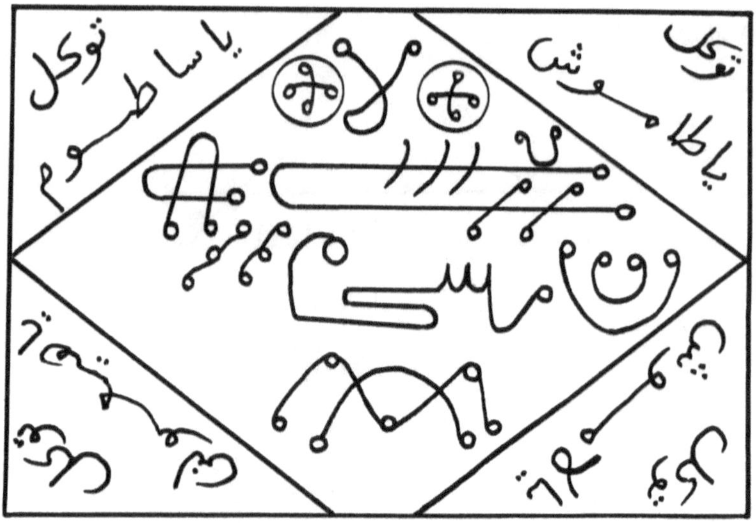

And this is the conjuration:

> *Ḥanūsh, Ḥanūsh, Ṭanūsh, Ṭanūsh, 'Anūsh, 'Anūsh, Shālshamūsh, Shālshamūsh, Shālmūsh, Shālmūsh, Shāliūsh, Shāliūsh, Ṭamiūsh, Ṭamiūsh, Ṭahshūsh, Ṭahshūsh, Yūsh, Yūsh, Lairūsh, Lairūsh, Larūsh, Larūsh. Be commissioned, O Ṭamūsh, and you, O Sāṭūm, and you, O Hay'aush, and you, O Lāmūsh, to answer me and to do so-and-so by the right of what was recited to you from Heaven. Now! Quickly! Immediately!*

CONJURATION OF KING MAYMŪN

If you want to perform this operation, take a bowl made of brass and write the following figures on its inner rim. Do this on the first Sunday of a lunar month after the dawn prayer, and be purified (abluted).

Fill the bowl with water and place it before you so you can stare into it. Afterwards cover the bowl and recite the conjuration seven times, then remove the cover from the bowl and you will see the Sultan with his soldiers saying to you: 'Peace be upon you, O sir!' Respond with the greeting of peace.

Thereafter cover the bowl for a second time, recite the conjuration seven times, then uncover the bowl and you will see a throne made of red gold and, sitting upon it, a man with black eyes and black in colour; his name is King Maymūn. Greet him with: *Peace be with you!* And he will respond to you: 'And upon you peace, O sir! What is your need?' Ask him for anything, and if you want a servant, or if you want a way to conjure one, say: *I desire from God and then from you to be assisted in conjuration and informed of all news.*

When you want to proceed, cover the bowl and recite the conjuration seven times and burn an incense of aloeswood, amber, bakhoor al-Sudan, liquid storax, gum mastic and coriander seeds. Uncover the bowl and you will see seven kings, and each one of them will request conditions from you.

When you have learned the conditions, make a pact with them and they will answer you in whatever you wish. When you want to perform a conjuration by yourself, write the following on a bowl or other vessel, burn the incense, recite the conjuration, and the kings will descend and inform you of everything you want to know. If you continue with this, they will obey you in everything you desire. This is the conjuration:

Shūsh, Shūsh, Ghūsh, Ghūsh, Mahtūsh, Mahtūsh, Maitatūsh, Maitatūsh, Ayhamūsh, Shamhalakh, Ayhamūsh, Shamhalakh, O Haitalab. Have no peace for a moment until you come to my abode in a blink of an eye, appear to me, and do what I command you. Aqṭalūl,[41] *Thal, Akhnāṭūa, Yanuāmi, Hadhah, Ṣabad, Bad'a, Halūt, Hūt, Dai'aut, Hā, Hai, Yanshamā, Hailūt.*

Answer to your summons, O spirits, so that you are unable to move

41 In another transcript, this is given as Aqtaul.

on your own until you come in a blink of an eye, appear, and do what I command by the right of these names, and the great crushing and destruction of those who do not obey them. Obey, submit, and appear before you are forced by the call and the end of the word![42] *Now! Quickly! Immediately! May the blessings of Allah be upon you! By the right of Ahiā, Sharāhiā, Adonai, Aṣbaot, El, Shadai, Shamakh, the Exalted above all that is blessed, He is Supreme above His servants. Hurry, Quickly! At once! Descend! May the blessings of Allah be upon you! Descend, by the might of Allah and his power, and what was done by the pen of Allah, the best of Allah's creation, Muhammad bin Abdullah, may Allah grant him peace!*[43]

This is the seal with the figures:

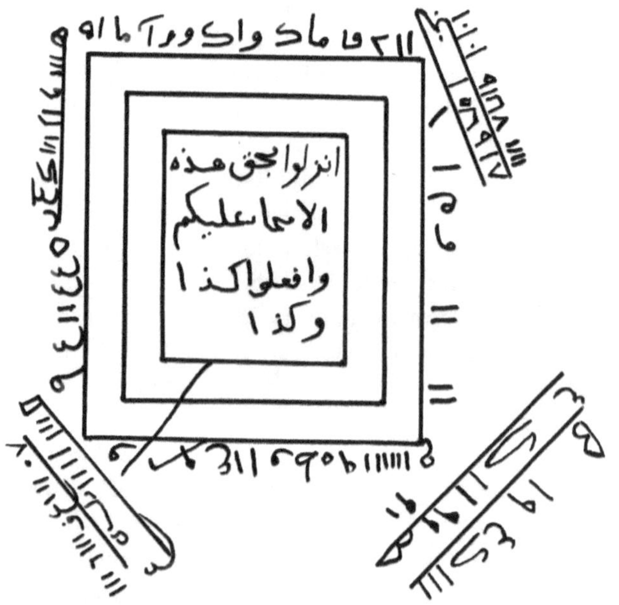

42 'The end of the word' means the end of the speech (the call). Before you finish the last word of the call they must submit.
43 According to Islam the book of universe (the Qur'ān) is written by the pen of Allah's 'Power.'

And this is the dismissal:

> *Say: O Allah! Owner of Sovereignty! Thou givest sovereignty unto whom Thou wilt, and Thou withdrawest sovereignty from whom Thou wilt. Thou exaltest whom Thou wilt, and Thou abasest whom Thou wilt. In Thy hand is the good. Lo! Thou art Able to do all things.*
>
> *Thou causest the night to pass into the day, and Thou causest the day to pass into the night. And Thou bringest forth the living from the dead, and Thou bringest forth the dead from the living. And Thou givest sustenance to whom Thou choosest, without stint.*[44]

Thereafter say:

> *I send you away! I send you away! I send you away! Allah turns your hearts. May the blessings of Allah be upon you!*

THE MANDAL OF NAHUIL

If you want to perform this mandal by yourself, take a white dish and write the following seal on it, then pour olive oil over it and place the dish before you. You should wear clean clothes, be purified and in solitude.

Burn incense of gum sandarac, benzoin and frankincense, and recite the conjuration until the dish starts spinning of its own accord before you. Look inside it and you will see the servant standing there. Say to him: *Peace be upon you, O servant!* He will reply by greeting you with peace. Ask him: *What is your name?* He will reply: 'My name is Nahuil.' Tell him: *O, Nahuil, I want you to inform me about such-and-such a theft and tell me where the stolen goods are, or about the location of such-and-such a treasure, and whether buried goods are present or not, or about the whereabouts of works of magic.*[45] *Answer me truthfully!*

44 Sūrat Āl 'Imrān: 26–27.

45 Most of the malicious works of magic (curses, hexes, evil spells) in Islamic occultism are made through some carrier (a talisman, a mixture of ingredients, bones, etc.) that should be placed or buried in a hidden place (such as a

If you are asking about a theft, a jinnī will appear in the shape of the thief, walking before you to lead you to the location of the goods. If you are asking him about buried goods, he will present the guardian of the treasure or the treasure trove to you. The guardian will address you. Ask him: *O guardian, what are your conditions if I want to take this treasure or these buried goods?* He will state his conditions to you. If you accept them, he will rise from the place of the treasure. Take what you require of him. And if you are asking about works of magic, a servant walking before you will lead you, to show you the place of the buried magic. Recite the conjuration, and Allah knows best.

This is the conjuration:

In the Name of Allah, the Most Beneficent, the Most Merciful. I conjure you, O spiritual beings and luminous bodies of pure fairness, they are angel Kushiā'īl and angel Nuqiā'īl, and angel Salumiā'īl, and angel Raqhiā'īl, and angel N'amiā'īl, and angel Sahriā'īl. Be commissioned, O ye angels, by the right of what He said unto (heaven) and unto the earth: Come both of you, willingly or loth. They said: We come, obedient.[46]

Be commissioned, O servants of these names: Kafaf, Lafaf, Nafaf, Lahfaf, Malhafaf, Nahulafaf, Kalfahaf, Talkahfalaf. Come, O servants, to my abode and inform me of what I am asking you. And lo! that verily is a tremendous oath, if ye but knew.[47]

Hurry! Quickly! At once! May the blessings of Allah be upon you!

grave), so that, once the spell is done, the only way to break it is to discover the location of the buried carrier, to extract it and to destroy it, in order to negate its evil power.

46 Sūrat Fuṣṣilat: 11.

47 Sūrat al-Wāqi'ah: 76.

This is the seal that should be written in the dish:

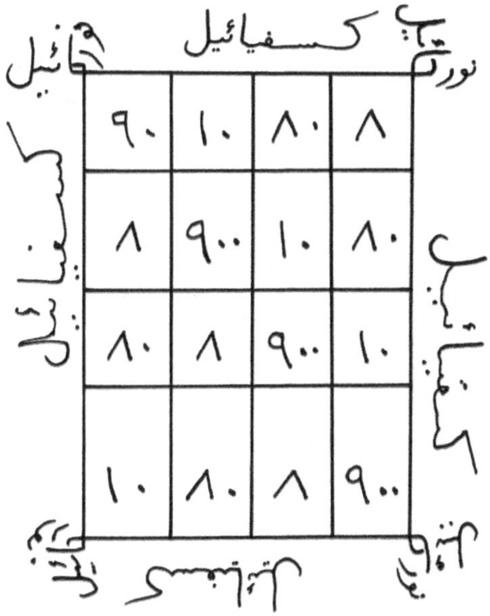

3

JINN WORKINGS AND EVOCATION RITES

Know, God bless you, O seeker, as I examined a manuscript with secret symbols, that I found within it these twelve workings of the jinn. They contain Suryani conjurations, and their secret is excellent and revolves around the ʿafārīt of the jinn and the spiritual kings.

THE FIRST WORKING

Fast for forty days in solitude. During this period eat only unsalted foods, such as barley bread and black raisins, and recite this conjuration one hundred times after each obligatory prayer:

> *O Banūkh and Dardamūkh, answer and hasten, you and your descendants, by the right of Saʿamāt, Shamʾawʾa, Barhūt, Barhīn, Asḥīm, and do, O ye aides, what I command you in the creation of love, separation, harm, fetching women, unearthing treasures and bringing news! Wheresoever ye may be, Allāh will bring you all together. Lo! Allāh is Able to do all things.*[1]

> يا بنوخ ودردموخ أجيبوا وتجلوا انتم وذرياتكم بحق سعماط شمعوع برهوت برهين اسحيم وافعلوا ايتها الاعوان ما امرتكم من الخدمة من محبة او فراق او تسليط وجلب النساء وفتح الكنوز وجلب الاخبار أينما تكونوا يأت بكم الله جميعا إن الله على كل شيء قدير

Thereafter write the conjuration out every day, dissolve it in water, and drink it at sunset. When you complete the fortieth day a servant will appear before you in the shape of a lion. Do not be afraid of him and continue with the conjuration. He will reappear in the form of a black slave, holding a red stone in his hand. Ask him to give it to you. Whenever you look at the stone and recite the conjuration, he will appear to fulfill your desire.

1 Sūrat al-Baqarah: 148.

THE SECOND WORKING

Fast for nine days and retreat to a cave far away from human habitation and do not eat anything except for sweet food such as fruits. Recite the conjuration one hundred and seventy times after each obligatory prayer and one thousand times before going to sleep. On the ninth day a servant will appear to you in the shape of a frog. Ask him to fetch women, to bring magic, for love or separation, to send jinn to cause harm or fever, or for the destruction of an oppressor. He will give you his seal in the form of a white stone. When you have this stone, suffumigate it with frankincense, and the jinnī will come to accomplish your desires.

During the nine days of recitation you should burn bakhoor al-Sudan and bdellium resin. And during the fasting of the first working, gum benzoin, gum mastic and liquid storax.

This is the conjuration:

Come, O Dardyail, upon the 'ifrīt Shamriad[2] *by the right of Ah, Ah, Yah, Yah, Huwa, Huwa, Allah the Only One, O Banūkh, and O Sh'ayqid, and O Sh'arqabad, come by the right of Samraad and Tabraad and 'Awuj and Taighub and Faghugh!*

THE THIRD WORKING

Of Shams Al-Qaramīd, daughter of King Al-Abeyaḍ

She is a jinnīya from among the daughters of the seven jinn kings. If you want to summon her, fast for twelve days and retire to a desolate place far away from clamour and the city. During this period do not eat anything besides barley bread and olive oil, and do not neglect to perform ritual ablution of your body and to burn an incense of gum mastic, liquid storax and spikenard every day. Read the conjuration seventy times after each obligatory prayer:

2 This means that the angel will descend upon the ifrīt, as a means of compelling him to obey.

I conjure you with the Suryani adjuration, by the one with the appealing figure and the attractive look and the beauty which will cover her body if she lets her pretty hair down, and a pillar of light will emanate from her if she smiles. Come to me, to love me and be at my service, O thou Fadilah the Flying. Where are your companions, Maymūna, and Yaquta, and Zuwayla, and Fatima from the clouds, and Ruqaya, daughter of Al-Aḥmar, and Yalusha, daughter of Shamradayail? Come, O daughters of the jinn kings, Sham'aat and Danhiu and Barghut, Anainur, Mazjal, Tarqab, do as you are commanded!

When you complete the required period, a giant snake will appear before you. Do not be afraid of it. The snake will wrap itself around your neck. Continue reciting the conjuration until it goes away. Then the daughters of the jinn will appear, all dressed in red silk and rubies, holding in their hands plates filled with gold and coins and they will say to you: 'Take these, O so-and-so!' Ignore them and they will disappear. Thereafter a white woman will appear to you with an undulating walk, covered in pomegranate blossoms, with golden bracelets on her wrists, and emerald anklets set with red and green rubies on her feet. And with her will be her servants, each one of them almost as beautiful as her. They will sweep and tidy up the place for the daughter of the jinn king. Then she will greet you with peace and you will hear her longing voice that no one is able to resist.

She will ask you to marry her. If you agree you won't be able to reach the loins of a human woman for intercourse. This means, if you marry the jinnīya you cannot marry a human woman. Afterwards state your demands to the jinnīya for whatever you wish, such as acceptance from all living beings[3] and the ability to subjugate them. She is powerful in this dominion.

3 Acceptance by means of being charming to anyone, so that people will love you as if you were a celebrity or a leader who has great authority and can intimidate people.

THE FOURTH WORKING

This is a brief working. The one who wants to perform it should fast for seven days, starting on the first Thursday of the lunar month. Write the conjuration on your palm and recite it one thousand times after each obligatory prayer. On the seventh day the servant will appear to you in the form of a thin serpent or a turtle. When you see him, burn an incense of red sandalwood, asphodel sap and anastatica leaves for him. This is an incense to subjugate the kings to you.

This is the conjuration:

Anainūr, Barhayā, Asmīm, Nahsh, come, O Burqān the ‘Ifrīt and O Blue Maymūn, and do what I command you!

انينور برهيا اسميم نهش اقبل يا برقان العفريت ويا ميمون الازرق وافعلوا ما امرتكم

When the servant appears, recite the conjuration until he takes the form of a black slave: this is the Blue Maymūn. Command him to serve you in bringing magic, arousing love between men and women, causing haemorrhage and illness, and finding buried treasures.

THE FIFTH WORKING

Read these names ten thousand times every day whilst in the desert, and bring incense of gum benzoin and frankincense with you. Burn the incense every day before sleep and, when you complete the twentieth day, a tall black slave will stand before you. His head will reach to the sky and his feet will touch the earth. Demand from him the ring on his hand and he will give it to you. Whenever you recite the names, compel the servant by his name, which is Shamtun Al-Ghalam, in works for bringing love, arousing a woman, tying a tongue, causing haemorrhage or illness, for dispersion, for eviction and subjugation of the jinn, for separation, and for the destruction of an oppressor. He will accomplish it in the fastest time.

These are the names:

Tashhamītha, Tam and Tabum, Ashim.

Learn the worth of these names and what they bring to you.

THE SIXTH WORKING

This is the working of King Al-Aḥmar, the ruler of Tuesday. Clean your clothes and purify your body. Go out to a desolate place far away from the houses of men. Fast for twenty-eight days and recite the conjuration twenty-eight times after each obligatory prayer. On the last day, write the conjuration on red paper and hang it in front of you on a thread of red silk.

The king of the working will appear before you in the shape of a red horse at the head of a great army. He will greet you in peace. Respond to him likewise. He will ask you what is your desire. Tell him that you want him to turn paper into silver, fetch women, cause illness and harm, evict jinn, win hearts and love, bring magic, and discover and unearth treasures. He will accept your requests and impart his own conditions to you in return. If you accept them, proceed to your work.

This is the conjuration:

Sarnūd and Ṭaiūd and Ṭaghugh and Faghūgh, come, O Aḥmar, you and your soldiers, to be at my service and council.

By those who set the ranks in battle order and those who drive away (the wicked) with reproof and those who read (the Word) for a reminder, Lo! thy Lord is surely One; Lord of the heavens and of the earth and all that is between them, and Lord of the sun's risings. Lo! We have adorned the lowest heaven with an ornament, the planets; With security from every froward devil. They cannot listen to the Highest Chiefs for they are pelted from every side, Outcast, and theirs is a perpetual torment; Save him who snatcheth a fragment, and there pursueth him a piercing flame. Then ask them (O Muhammad): Are they stronger as a creation, or those (others) whom We have created? Lo! We created them of plastic clay.[4] *And the trumpet is blown and lo! from the graves they hie unto their Lord, crying: Woe upon us! Who hath raised us from our place of sleep? This is that which the Beneficent did promise, and the messengers spoke truth. It is but one Shout, and behold them brought together before Us!*[5] *and (We gave him) certain of the jinn who worked before him by permission of his Lord. And such of them as deviated from Our command, them We caused to taste the punishment of flaming fire.*[6]

سرنود وطيود وطاغوغ وفاغوغ أقبل يا أحمر أنت وجنودك الى خدمتي والى مجلسي بحق والصافات صفا فالزاجرات زجرا فالتاليات ذكرا إن إلهكم لواحد رب السماوات والأرض وما بينهما ورب المشارق إنا زينا السماء الدنيا بزينة الكواكب وحفظا من كل شيطان مارد لا يسمعون إلى الملإ الأعلى ويقذفون من كل جانب دحورا ولهم عذاب واصب إلا من خطف الخطفة فأتبعه شهاب ثاقب فاستفتهم أهم أشد خلقا أم من خلقنا إنا خلقناهم من طين لازب ونفخ في الصور فإذا هم من الأجداث إلى ربهم ينسلون الوا يا ويلنا من بعثنا من مرقدنا هذا ما وعد الرحمن وصدق المرسلون إن كانت إلا صيحة واحدة فإذا هم جميع لدينا محضرون ومن الجن من يعمل بين يديه بإذن ربه ومن يزغ منهم عن أمرنا نذقه من عذاب السعير

The incense for this working is red sandalwood.

THE SEVENTH WORKING

Fast for twenty-one days in a desolate place and be purified. Recite *Sūrat ash-Shams* five hundred times:

By the sun and his brightness, And the moon when she followeth him, And the day when it revealeth him, And the night when it enshroudeth him, And the heaven and Him who built it, And the earth and Him who spread it, And a soul and Him who perfected it And inspired it (with conscience of) what is wrong for it and (what is) right for it. He is

4 Sūrat aṣ-Ṣāffāt: 1–11.
5 Sūrat Yā'-Sīn: 51–53.
6 Sūrat Saba': 12.

indeed successful who causeth it to grow, and he is indeed a failure who stunteth it. (The tribe of) Thamūd denied (the truth) in their rebellious pride, when the basest of them broke forth and the messenger of Allah said: It is the she-camel of Allah, so let her drink! But they denied him, and they hamstrung her, so Allah doomed them for their sin and razed (their dwellings). He dreadeth not the sequel (of events).

And after each hundredth repetition say this conjuration once:

O Bardamūsh, come by the right of Shamat, Kamāt and Nūd and Sarhūsh and Banūkh, arrive, O servant of this blessed sūrat, and do what I command you, such as transforming money,[7] fetching women, winning hearts, and causing illness and expulsion from houses by the right of the knowledge of what was and what will be!

When you complete the required number of days, recite the previous conjuration five hundred times. Burn an incense of gum mastic, liquid storax and bakhoor al-Sudan. At the completion of the repetitions, the servant will appear to you in the form of a white man in a green robe holding a sword in his hand. He will ask you what is your desire. Answer him. He will give you a ring made of red copper on which is written the Greatest Name of God in Suryani. Whenever you state your need compel the servant by reading the sūrat and the conjuration and he will appear and accomplish it.

7 Transforming money is an advanced magical practice that is intended to turn plain paper into banknotes or ordinary rocks into precious metals or stones (comparable to the power of the philosopher's stone). It is done only through the help of powerful jinn and its effect doesn't last long; for example, when you spend the enchanted money, the banknotes usually turn back into paper on the following day.

THE EIGHTH WORKING

Fast for ten days beginning on a Friday. Eat only unsalted barley bread and black raisins. Recite the conjuration one hundred and forty times after each obligatory prayer:

> *Sarbūd, Banūkh, 'Aajaul and Taimūl, come, O Aba Al-Kalb,*[8] *and do what I command you by the right of these Suryani names! And lo! that verily is a tremendous oath, if ye but knew.*[9]

When you complete the required number of days, burn an incense of gum ammoniac with bakhoor al-Sudan and recite the conjuration three thousand times. The servant will appear to you in the form of a dog. You can make a pact with him for winning over hearts, for causing love between men and women, for separation, for illness, for exorcism, for fever and haemorrhage, for bringing magic, for unearthing treasures, and so forth.

THE NINTH WORKING

This is the working of King Al-Abeyaḍ. Fast for forty days, eating only permissible food, and do not approach women during this period but be in retreat in your house. Recite the conjuration one hundred times and *Sūrat al-Jinn* three times after each obligatory prayer, and burn incense of bdellium resin and aloeswood.

This is the conjuration:

> *I conjure you, O King Al-Abeyaḍ, come, you and your servants, by the right of Mashrabū'a and Shāmūl and Darūṭ. Do what I command you by the right of Nawdaj and Sharbālīt and Sharhām!*

أقسمت عليك أيها الملك الأبيض أقبل أنت وخدامك بحق مشربوع وشامول ودروط
أفعل ما أمرتك بحق نودج وشربليط وشرهام

8 Father of the Dog.
9 Sūrat al-Wāqi'ah: 76.

Say (O Muhammad): It is revealed unto me that a company of the Jinn gave ear, and they said: Lo! it is a marvellous Qur'an, Which guideth unto righteousness, so we believe in it and we ascribe no partner unto our Lord. And (we believe) that He – exalted be the glory of our Lord! – hath taken neither wife nor son, And that the foolish one among us used to speak concerning Allah an atrocious lie.And lo! we had supposed that humankind and Jinn would not speak a lie concerning Allah – And indeed (O Muhammad) individuals of humankind used to invoke the protection of individuals of the Jinn, so that they increased them in revolt (against Allah); And indeed they supposed, even as ye suppose, that Allah would not raise anyone (from the dead) – And (the Jinn who had listened to the Qur'an said): We had sought the heaven but had found it filled with strong warders and meteors.And we used to sit on places (high) therein to listen. But he who listeneth now findeth a flame in wait for him; And we know not whether harm is boded unto all who are in the earth, or whether their Lord intendeth guidance for them. And among us there are righteous folk and among us there are far from that. We are sects having different rules. And we know that we cannot escape from Allah in the earth, nor can we escape by flight. And when we heard the guidance, we believed therein, and whoso believeth in his Lord, he feareth neither loss nor oppression. And there are among us some who have surrendered (to Allah) and there are among us some who are unjust. And whoso hath surrendered to Allah, such have taken the right path purposefully. And as for those who are unjust, they are firewood for hell. If they (the idolaters) tread the right path, We shall give them to drink of water in abundance That We may test them thereby, and whoso turneth away from the remembrance of his Lord; He will thrust him into ever-growing torment. And the places of worship are only for Allah, so pray not unto anyone along with Allah. And when the slave of Allah stood up in prayer to Him, they crowded on him, almost stifling.

Say (unto them, O Muhammad): I pray unto Allah only, and ascribe unto Him no partner. Say: Lo! I control not hurt nor benefit for you. Say: Lo! none can protect me from Allah, nor can I find any refuge beside Him. (Mine is) but conveyance (of the truth) from Allah, and His mes-

sages; and whoso disobeyeth Allah and His messenger, lo! his is fire of hell, wherein such dwell for ever. Till (the day) when they shall behold that which they are promised (they may doubt); but then they will know (for certain) who is weaker in allies and less in multitude. Say (O Muhammad, unto the disbelievers): I know not whether that which ye are promised is nigh, or if my Lord hath set a distant term for it. (He is) the Knower of the Unseen, and He revealeth unto none His secret, Save unto every messenger whom He hath chosen, and then He maketh a guard to go before him and a guard behind him that He may know that they have indeed conveyed the messages of their Lord. He surroundeth all their doings, and He keepeth count of all things.[10]

When you have completed the required number of days, go out to a desolate place, taking frankincense with you. Draw a circle on the ground and write the conjuration in its centre. Recite the conjuration until you see soldiers approaching. Make a pact with them for what you desire.

THE TENTH WORKING

This working is from the secret manuscript of Shaykh Al-Amoua. Write the Suryani conjuration on a green wick, and burn it in oil on the seventeenth night.[11] During this period, be in retreat and recite the conjuration three hundred times after each obligatory prayer and burn black nadd incense continually.

When you complete the required number of days, light the wick in a new green lamp filled with olive oil. Recite the conjuration and burn the incense after Isha', the night prayer. The servant will appear to you in the shape of a large serpent. Continue with the recitation and he will go away, reappearing in the form of a wolf that speaks to you. Make an agreement with him for what you desire.

10 Sūrat al-Jinn.

11 This means that you should write the conjuration on a piece of a green fabric and then twist it as a wick and burn it in an oil lamp.

He is an ʿifrīt who reveals the jinn's treasures. His name is the Black Zarqād and he will do as you command. This is the conjuration:

Ṣabrūḥ, Yankab, Maihūb, Mashjarat, come, O Black Zarqād, and do what I command you!

صبروح ينكب ميهوب مشجرة أقبل يا أسود الزرقاد وافعل ما أمرتك

THE ELEVENTH WORKING

This is the working of the celestial spirits. Fast for forty-nine days and be in retreat, and recite these Suryani names one thousand times after each obligatory prayer:

Nud, Jabrud, Washwash, Almighty in His kingship.

Every night before you go to sleep burn an incense of frankincense, gum benzoin, liquid storax, gum mastic, aloeswood and cloves, and recite the names one thousand times. When you complete the required number of days, you will see the celestial spirits. Ask them for obedience in anything and they will respond to you.

THE TWELFTH WORKING

Of Aba Yaqub Al-Aḥmar

Fast for thirty days, beginning on a Tuesday, and recite the conjuration seventy times after each obligatory prayer. On the last day, recite the conjuration one thousand times and burn incense of red muqul,[12] aloeswood, red gum benzoin and musk.

This is the conjuration:

Come, O Aba Yaqub Al-Aḥmar, you and your armies, and do what I

12 Red muqul is an incense, most probably a resin, since blue muqul is bdellium gum, but I don't know what this red one is.

command you by the right of Sam, Sam, Qudus, Rash, Haimal, by the right of he Who said unto (heaven) and unto the earth: Come both of you, willingly or loth. They said: We come, obedient.[13]

Samhar'a, Namuh, Shamtar'a. And when We inclined toward thee (Muhammad) certain of the Jinn, who wished to hear the Qur'an and, when they were in its presence, said: Give ear! and, when it was finished, turned back to their people, warning. They said: O our people! Lo! we have heard a scripture which hath been revealed after Moses, confirming that which was before it, guiding unto the truth and a right road. O our people! respond to Allah's summoner and believe in Him. He will forgive you some of your sins and guard you from a painful doom. And whoso respondeth not to Allah's summoner he can no wise escape in the earth, and ye (can find) no protecting friends instead of Him. Such are in error manifest.[14] *By the right of Yah, Yah, And lo! that verily is a tremendous oath, if ye but knew.*[15]

On the thirtieth day the servant will appear to you as a rider on a red mule. Make an agreement with him for what you desire, such as bringing money, evicting jinn, fetching women, unearthing treasures and so forth.

13 Sūrat Fuṣṣilat: 11.
14 Sūrat al-Aḥqāf: 29–32.
15 Sūrat al-Wāqi'ah: 76.

Know that these servants are great aerial kings. Demand from them what you desire from the spiritual work. If you want them to manifest to you, fast for seven days, eating no meat or animal products. Write the seal on a clean plate every day, dissolve it in water, and drink it. Also write the seal, suffumigate it every day, and wear it on you.

This is the invocation:

He is the First and the Last, and the Outward and the Inward; and He is Knower of all things.[16] *Glory be to Him and High is He! He is Allah, creator of Dardyail and Samsamail and Ruqiail and Nuriail and Talhakfiail and Shamkhiail and Shadkhiail. Answer, O noble Mayamin that God created in the air.*[17] *By the right of the Light of the Lights and the Secret of the Secrets, aid me in what I ask and demand of you, and command you for everything by the right of the Lord of all things and He who is all Knowing, and by the right of the names that descended and ascended with you, Ah, Ah, Huwail, Huwail, El, El, Elohim, Elohim, Yah, Yah, Namuh, Namuh, Ahia, Sharahia, Adonai, Asbaot, El, Shadai. He is the Lord of the highest light and Lord of the upper and lower abodes. Unto Him belongeth whatsoever is in the heavens and whatsoever is in the earth, and whatsoever is between them, and whatsoever is beneath the sod. And if thou speakest aloud, then lo! He knoweth the secret (thought) and (that which is yet) more hidden. Allah! There is no God save Him. His are the most beautiful names.*[18]

Answer, O Faqtash, and you, O Tarhash, and you, O Haqial, and you, O Barjual, and you, O Khandash, and you, O Naikal, and you, O Shamradal, come and fulfill my request which is so-and-so. May Allah bestow his blessings upon you.

16 Sūrat al-Ḥadīd: 3.

17 God created the Seven Mayamin in the realm of the element Air.

18 Sūrat Ṭā-Hā: 6–8.

Know that the response to this invocation is fast and it is powerful over the lower spirits and these are its applications:

THE FIRST APPLICATION

To bring back an absent person. Write the seal on an article of the target's clothing with the commission[19] written around it in separated letters, mixed with the Letters of the Air,[20] along with the target's name and a commission of yearning for the country he left. Then wash yourself and be pure. Take a suitable candle for the work and inscribe the names and the commission on it. Afterwards suffumigate the candle with the invocation's incense[21] and also suffumigate the item of the target's clothing, wrap the candle with the clothing, light both the candle and the incense, and recite the invocation twenty-one times for each letter.[22] The missing one will come directly, without straying from the road.

THE SECOND APPLICATION

To expel a bad neighbour. Do not perform this operation except against an oppressor or an immoral person. Write the seal with the petition on a scapula taken from a dead dog on Saturday in the hour of Saturn. Write it with onion and garlic water and black ink. Suffumigate it with gum sandarac and sulphur and recite the invocation nightly twenty-one times for three days. Afterwards bury it, or pulverise it and sprinkle the dust with vinegar in the house of the neighbour, and indeed he will be expelled and he will never return as long as the scapula is buried, or unless you annul the operation.

19 The commission is the written command, such as: 'I order you to bring me so-and-so!'.

20 In Arabic magic, all twenty-eight letters of the alphabet are divided into four groups of seven letters each, each group corresponding to one of the four elements. The Letters of Air are: ظ ث ق س ك ز ج

21 The incense is not stated explicitly in the text here, but it is given and described in the twelfth application.

22 The wording is not clear in the original. My opinion is that it refers to the seven Letters of the Air. So you recite the invocation 21×7 times (147 in total).

THE THIRD APPLICATION

To release an imprisoned person. This is from the curiosities.[23] Take seven stones from a canyon and write one of the names of the Seven Mayamin on each of them. Carry them with you, and by night take a brazier, put the incense on it and recite the invocation twenty-one times over the first stone and then place it in the fire. Do the same with the rest of the stones and, on the eighth night, recite the invocation with the commission and throw the stones at the corners of the prison. Also draw the seal which should be worn by the imprisoned person. He will indeed be pardoned and released. Repeat the procedure until it succeeds.

THE FOURTH APPLICATION

To curb the speech of the ruler during an audience.[24] Draw the seal on a piece of red wax and write the Iqama prayer call around it. Write it with a copper needle, or a reed pen with a copper nib, and recite the invocation over it, bathe it with incense during the day on which you write it and on the day of your audience. After this is done, wear it about you, and proceed to your audience with the ruler. Your reputation will grow and he will fulfill what you require of him.

THE FIFTH APPLICATION

For stoning the house of whomsoever you wish. Go to a river near the city where you will perform the operation and take twenty-one pebbles from it and recite the invocation once over each of them. Then take blood from a red rooster or, failing that, from a black pigeon. Thereafter write the name of each of the Seven Mayamin on three pebbles. Do this at the end of the lunar month in the hour

23 'The curiosities' is a common Arabic expression that also means wonder or peculiarity. The author is saying that the ritual is like a wonder, or like something from those tales and legends of wonders.

24 When you go before the ruler, he may be angry or arrogant towards you, but through this spell you will make him unable to speak ill against you, and force him to be well disposed toward you.

of Saturn. Bathe the pebbles with the incense and put them on the left side of your lap and recite the invocation twenty-one times over each of them. When this is done, go by night to the intended house and bury the pebbles near it and it will be stoned. If you want to stop this, remove the pebbles and erase the names with water.

THE SIXTH APPLICATION

For love and arousal. Write the seal with the blood of a white dove on a plate made of yellow brass. Likewise write the names along with your desire on a candle and place it in the centre of the seal. Then light it and recite the invocation twenty-one times every night until the desired person is aroused. And know that this application gives a fast response.

THE SEVENTH APPLICATION

To send the Seven Mayamin. Write the seal on red paper or a plate of red copper, then burn the incense and recite the invocation twenty-one times after each obligatory prayer for one or three days. If you wrote it on paper, proof it with white wax and put it inside a reed and seal the openings with red wax, then hang it in the open air facing the target's location. If you wrote it on a copper plate, bury it in a fireplace under a small fire. In the statement of intent say: *Answer, O thee noble Mayamin, and frighten so-and-so with* (state the kind of fears) *until he comes humiliated and defeated; and accomplish or give me so-and so!*

THE EIGHTH APPLICATION

To stop a person from leaving. Write the seal on a plate of old lead in the last hour of Mars in a lunar month. Suffumigate it and recite the invocation over the plate twenty-one times. Bury it at the city gate and the person will not be able to depart. If you recite the invocation seven times after each obligatory prayer for three days the person will not even be able to leave his own house. Fear God the Almighty.

THE NINTH APPLICATION

To sicken an enemy and oppressor. Make an effigy from red wax then drill a hole in its belly. Take a little dust from the target, write the seal, wrap the dust in it, and place it in the belly of the effigy, then close the opening. Write the first name of the Seven Mayamin on the right hand of the figurine, and the second name on its left hand, and the third on its right leg, and the fourth on its left leg, and the fifth on its chest, and the sixth on its back and the seventh on its head. Perform the operation on Saturday in the hour of Saturn. Thereafter suffumigate the effigy and recite the invocation twenty-one times over each name and every time stab it with a thorn while saying the target's name. Likewise do this with the rest of the seven names. Know that the servant of this invocation who operates in the working is not mentioned in the seal and the invocation because the shaykhs of this science are afraid to reveal it to the ignorant. His name is Dahmush. In order to complete this operation, break the limb that you want to damage and the target will become sick. Fear God. If you want to forgive the target and annul the work, remove the written seal from the figurine's belly, extract the thorns and recite the invocation twenty-one times with a request for cessation.

THE TENTH APPLICATION

Also for causing sickness. Write the seal on yellow paper with black ink and write the invocation around it. Suffumigate it with the incense in the last hour of Saturn in the lunar month and recite the invocation twenty-one times over it. Thereafter take a sheep's heart, from a ram if the target is a man, or from a ewe if the target is a woman. Wax the paper seal, split the heart, and place the seal in its centre. Sew up the opening with red thread using an unused iron needle. Hang the heart in the open air and suffumigate it with the incense and recite the invocation over it twenty-one times, then hang the heart from a tree facing the target's location and they will be severely sickened. If you want to annul the work, remove the seal from the heart with a statement of dismissal.

THE ELEVENTH APPLICATION

To discover a treasure. This is from the greatest operations. Go to the nearest olive grove when the moon is in an Air sign and cut seven branches from the same tree, but do not cut them with an iron tool. Afterwards split the branches in half and inscribe a name of the Seven Mayamin with a request to Dahmush on each of them.[25] Then bind them together with a red silk or wool thread the length of a handspan or footprint. Make a retreat in a clean house for three days, burn the incense, and recite the invocation twenty- one times after each obligatory prayer. On the third day, separate the olive branches and spread them around the house. The answer will be given by the branches gathering in one place. If this does not happen, repeat the operation for seven days. When you receive the answer, take the branches with you and go to the place of the buried treasure and recite the invocation twenty-one times and it will be found and taken by you.

THE TWELFTH APPLICATION

Take powdered basil and powdered sulphur, mix them together with liquid storax, and recite the invocation over it twenty-one times. When you want to make someone or a group of people fall asleep, burn the incense and recite the invocation twenty-one times, and each time request Dahmush to perform the deed, gesture toward the targets, and they will fall asleep.

25 The instructions are not very clear here. I interpret them to mean that when you split the seven branches you write the name and the commission on all the halves, so you will have 14 branches with the same writing on them.

This is the seal of the invocation:

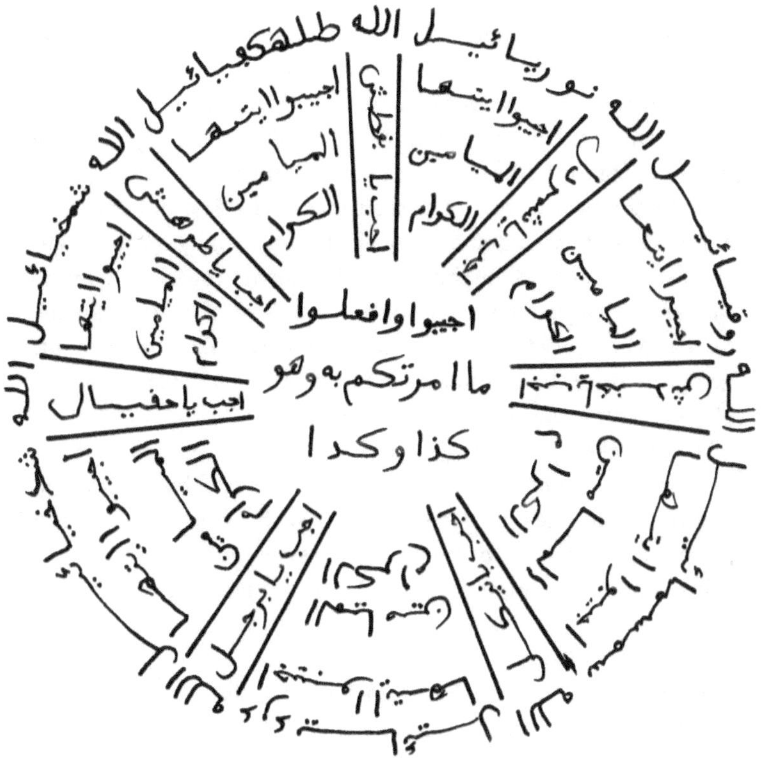

SUMMONING A WHISPERING JINNĪ

For reading private thoughts

If you want to know people's private thoughts, their secrets and intentions towards you, perform the following operation. The servant, whose name is Wash, will soon inform you.

Inscribe the talisman on a lead plate in the hour of Venus. Afterwards perform the operation for a period of fourteen days. Observe fasting during the first seven of them, and during the next seven recite the conjuration one hundred times in the day, and one thousand times in the night, and burn any sweet smelling incense. The sign of the answer will be that you will hear the voice of the jinnī in your ear, so that you may make a pact with him. Then take the talisman and bring it to your right ear. He will say: 'Yes, I am present.' Then pronounce the formula of the pact: *Inform me and make a pact with me to come at any time.*

He will make a pact with you and will reveal his real name to you. Afterwards whenever you wear the plate with his talisman and recite the names, he will attend saying: 'Wash,' which is the mark of his presence. He will inform you of whatever you ask him.

This is the conjuration that you should read during the seven days:

Kamsh, Kamsh, Hashhash, Hashhash, Kakash, Kakash, Shālīkh, Shālīkh, answer and attend, O servant of these names, and inform me about people's thoughts!

And you should read this one hundred times before each obligatory prayer during the seven days of the operation:

O Allah, O Allah, O Giver of Dishonour, O All-Knowing, O All-Aware, subjugate him to me in order to inform me of my demands, O Allah Lord of the Worlds!

This is the talisman:

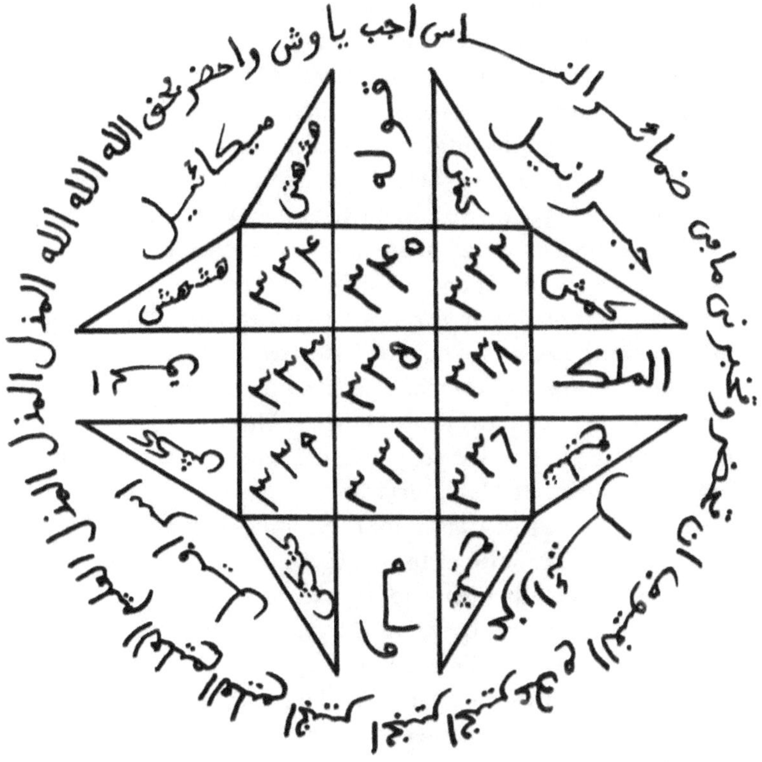

When you recite the formulas, suffumigate the talisman and contemplate it. It is from the wonders and curiosities copied from Mr. Al-Arabi, who inscribed the writing on a thin red board.

WORKING OF TARESH, THE KING OF THE RESIDENT JINN[26]

He is the ruler of all the resident jinn of the East and West. This king holds a great and mighty office, and all of the resident jinn are afraid of him, fear his power, and obey him by the permission of the almighty Allah. When you summon any resident jinnī and he tarries in coming to you or disobeys you, summon this noble king and command him to present the jinnī. If he does not appear instantly then he will be brought shivering before you, like a flame on a windy day. Command the king to do with him whatsoever you desire, whether expelling, beating, killing, imprisoning him, or otherwise.

When you want to employ this king, fast for seven days and recite the conjuration fifty-nine times each night. You will see horrors and frightening visions. Do not be afraid, strengthen your heart and your intention. You will see many people prostrating themselves on the ground and afterwards you will see the king coming towards you with his men. He will greet you in peace and he will ask you what is your desire. Tell him: *Submit to Allah and to these names, I request you to make a pact with me and to subjugate the resident jinn to me!* He will impart his conditions to you. If you accept them, you will become one who neither fears nor is touched by sorrow. There is another method of three days, found in an old transcript, most of it encoded in the Script of Hermes.[27]

The incense for the operation is frankincense, gum benzoin, coriander seeds and labdanum kneaded with rose water.

This is the conjuration:

Ashalat, Ashalat, Dahlusha, Dahlusha, Marsha, Marsha, 'Ausha, 'Ausha, Atha, Atha, Latshaithathata, Latshaithathata, Falfalainasha, Falfalainasha, Balthutha, Balthutha, Samsamun, Samsamun, Bahamush, Bahamush, Haiush, Haiush, Samsamun, Samsamun. O fine spirit,

26 You can also call resident jinn spiritual inhabitants, for they are jinn that live alongside humans in our homes.

27 The Script of Hermes is a magical script like the 'Passing the River' alphabet in Western occultism. The author notes that there is also another version of the ritual in another transcript that is encoded in this script.

virtuous king Taresh, king of the resident jinn, answer, come and obey by the right of these names and the obedience you owe them. Now, Now! Quickly, Quickly! Immediately, Immediately!

Completion of this operation.

THE REBUKE OF KING TARESH

If he is slow to come, recite these names twenty-three times, for they are the secret of his submission. He will come to you in a blink of an eye, if he is tardy he will burn. Recite:

Tabibah, Tabibah, Tabshish, Tabshish. Submit to Allah and to these names, O Taresh, answer and come. Quickly!

It has been completed and Allah knows best.

PROVEN EXPERIMENT OF A JINNĪ

This operation is for divining what is happening at each hour for good or ill, and for whatever you wish to know of your affairs, of treasure crypts, buried hoards, and other things. Recite these names one thousand times for three nights, and after each hundredth repetition say:

O Daimuta, show me, O Guide, and inform me, O All-Aware, and clarify to me, O Clear seeing one, and tell me, O Knower of the unseen, what is happening at this hour for good or ill.

These are the names that should be recited one thousand times:

The Guide, the All-Aware, the Clear-sighted, the Knower of the Unseen, Shamrush, Shamrush, Shahul, Shahul, Baidar, Baidar, 'Ainshar, 'Ainshar.

The incense for the operation is white costus and gum benzoin.

EMPLOYMENT OF A JINNĪ

For attraction, arousal and binding sleep

Recite the names one thousand times on a Saturday night in a toilet and burn the incense of the working, which is bakhoor al-Sudan.[28] The servant will appear to you in the form of a cat. Take some of his hairs, if you can, and burn them as incense. You will see people with no faces, but with eyes on the top of their heads, and with them will be a short man with many hands. Request to make a pact with him: by the white hand if you seek love, by the red hand if you seek destruction, by the green hand if you seek fulfilment of desires, or by the black hand if you seek works of evil.[29] Each hand has its own function, for whatever you need: ask him and greet him with peace. His incense is Indian maskhāṭar, mistletoe berries and Arabian boxthorn mixed with heartleaf iceplant's juice.[30]

These are the names:

Yahtash, Yahtash, Lakh, Lakh, Kagha, Kagha, Katah, Katah. Bend your necks to him, and submit your burdens to him. Whoever calls on him will not fail. Answer, O Sinjab, O son of the Gatekeeper, or be thrown into the blazing fire! Now! Quickly! Immediately!

WORKING OF THE SIX DAUGHTERS

The daughters are those of the queens of the jinn and under their governance are servants and aides, and none knows their number except Allah. If you want to employ them, write the following six names on your left palm. Enter the toilet and recite the six names one thousand times and burn the incense of the operation which is calamus, nigella, gum mastic, and styrax.

28 Some rituals are performed in a toilet or bathhouse, since it is considered to be a place that is inhabited by jinn.

29 It is not explained in the text how exactly you make the pact with the jinnī, but I assume that either you shake hands with him or, more probably, that the jinnī himself will reveal how to make the pact with him.

30 *Aptenia cordifolia.*

You will see the toilet enlarging and inside it appearing tents, cupolas, pavilions, soldiers, armies, weapons and horses of all breeds and colours. And you will see the six daughters seated upon thrones as queens, and be unable to tear your sight from them. Thereafter a servant from their escort will address you, saying to you: 'What is your desire?' Tell him your demands, saying: *I am a humble servant looking for your generosity, honour me with your grace!* He will reply: 'Do you want to be married?' If this suits you say: *Yes*; but be careful not to be hurt by her.[31]

Accept their conditions and stipulate what you want to them, such as fetching objects, bringing back a missing person, revealing the identity of a thief, snatching money from the hands of the Jews, fetching a beloved person, destroying adversaries, ruining oppressors, evicting an enemy, opening treasures, discovering hidden goods, and so forth. In brief, take a personal sign from them so that you can learn how to summon them with it. Allah is the Guide on the Right Path.

These are the names to recite:

Maridān, Maridān, Baridān, Baridān, Sharidān, Sharidān, Saridān, Saridān, Ṭahmalīn, Ṭahmalīn, Kahīmlīn, Kahīmlīn. Answer by the Lord of the fire and light, the shade and the heat, and by the places of the stars. And lo! that verily is a tremendous oath, if ye but knew.[32]

مريدان مريدان بريدان بريدان شريدان شريدان سريدان سريدان طهملين طهملين
كهيملين كهيملين أجيبوا برب النار والنور والظل والحرور وبمواقع النجوم وانه لقسم
لو تعلمون عظيم

31 In Arabic magic, it is known that when a human man takes a wife from among the jinn, he will never be able to sleep with a human woman again, and if he is not faithful to his jinnīya wife she will punish him and hurt him severely. She may even kill him out of jealousy.

32 Sūrat al-Wāqi'ah: 76.

WORKING OF MAYMŪN THE ABDUCTOR

This is for seizing the minds and snatching money from the hands of anyone you want, whether they are near or far away. Write the seal on a new piece of linen, and twist that like a wick and put it into a clay lamp filled with olive oil. Light the wick and recite the conjuration seventy-one times for a period of three nights. After that a smoke will appear to you, whirling around the brazier. Know that the answer is given for certain.

This is the conjuration:

Ashṭūkh, Ashṭūkh, Shaṭūkh, Shaṭūkh, ʿAbrūd, ʿAbrūd, Dairabūd, Dairabūd, Yarbūd, Yarbūd, Kankūsh, Kankūsh, Alātūsh, Alātūsh, ʿAuj, ʿAuj, Faiʾauj, Faiʾauj, Daiʾauj, Daiʾauj, ʿAuj, ʿAuj.

The commandment of Allah is always executed.[33] *Wheresoever ye may be, Allah will bring you all together. Lo! Allah is Able to do all things.*[34]

Answer, O Maymūn the Abductor, descend, go and snatch so-and-so quickly and swiftly by the right of: Lo! it is from Solomon,[35] *and it is for the Muslims. Hastily, willingly! Allah Lord of the Worlds.*

This is the seal:

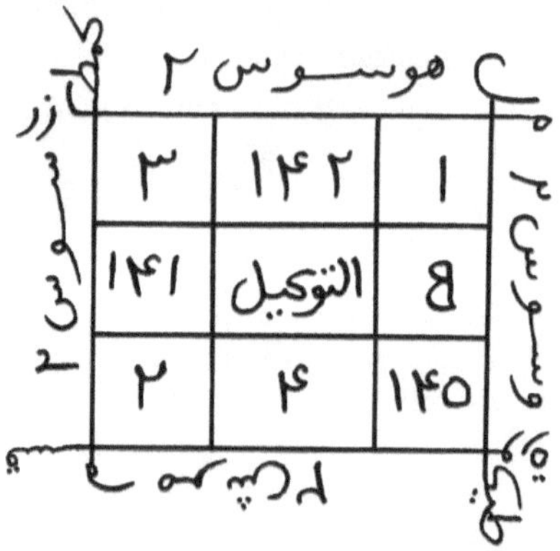

33 Sūrat an-Nisāʾ: 47.

34 Sūrat al-Baqarah: 148.

35 Sūrat an-Naml: 30.

IF YOU WANT TO FRATERNISE WITH THE PIOUS JINN

So that they will fulfill your needs and hasten to please you

Begin to fast on a Wednesday, and continue until the fourth Saturday following it. Then you should wash your body and clothing and recite *Sūrat al-Ikhlas* one thousand times daily, and *Sūrat Yā'-Sīn*, *Sūrat ad-Dukhān*, *Sūrat as-Sajdah* and *Sūrat al-Mulk* once every day. On Saturday afternoon, at the tenth hour, go into seclusion in an empty and clean place away from people. Take seven strips of paper, and write on the first:

وهو الذي يحيي ويميت وله اختلاف الليل والنهار

And He it is Who giveth life and causeth death, and His is the difference of night and day.[36]

On the second:

وإذا قضى أمرا فإنما يقول له كن فيكون

When He decreeth a thing, He saith unto it only: Be! and it is.[37]

On the third:

فسيكفيكهم الله وهو السميع العليم

and Allah will suffice thee (for defence) against them. He is the Hearer, the Knower.[38]

On the fourth:

ثم إذا دعاكم دعوة من الأرض إذا أنتم تخرجون

when He calleth you, lo! from the earth ye will emerge.[39]

36 Sūrat al-Mu'minūn: 80.
37 Sūrat al-Baqarah: 117.
38 Sūrat al-Baqarah: 137.
39 Sūrat ar-Rūm: 25.

On the fifth:

فإذا هم من الأجداث إلى ربهم ينسلون

and lo! from the graves they hie unto their Lord.[40]

On the sixth:

ونفخ في الصور فصعق من في السماوات ومن في الأرض إلا من شاء الله ثم نفخ فيه أخرى فإذا هم قيام ينظرون

And the trumpet is blown, and all who are in the heavens and the earth swoon away, save him whom Allah willeth. Then it is blown a second time, and behold them standing waiting![41]

And on the seventh:

يوم يخرجون من الأجداث سراعا فسيكفيكهم الله وهو السميع العليم

The day when they come forth from the graves in haste.[42] *When He decreeth a thing, He saith unto it only: Be! and it is.*[43]

Thereafter pray four *rak'ah*, the first one with *Sūrat al-Fātiḥah*, the second with *Sūrat Yā'-Sīn*, the third with *Sūrat ad-Dukhān*, and the fourth with sūrats *Al-Fātiḥah*, *As-Sajdah* and *Al-Mulk*, and say at the end of each prostration:

Glory be to Him who is clad in honour and dignity, glory be to Him who is generous amidst the glory that surrounds Him, glory be to Him whose knowledge encompasses everything, glory be to Him, for there is nothing that behoves glorification, except for Him, glory be to Him, for when He intends a thing, His Command is, 'Be!' and it is, glory be to Him, for when He intends a thing, it comes into being, and whatever He does not intend will never be, glory be to Him for His kindness and favour, glory

40 Sūrat Yā'-Sīn: 51.
41 Sūrat az-Zumar: 68.
42 Sūrat al-Ma'ārij: 43.
43 Sūrat al-Baqarah: 117.

be to Him for His wisdom and patience, glory be to Him for His might and grace, glory be to Him, the Lord of the Throne, the Tablet, the Pen and the Light!

Then raise your head and say:

O Allah, I ask You by the glory of Your Throne and the Mercy of Your Book and Your Greatest Name and Your Generous and Most honourable face and Your perfect words, to subordinate an aide to me from among the pious jinn to help me in whatever I desire for my worldly needs.

Then there will appear before you seven figures of the most notable and greatest jinn, who will submit to you and follow your orders. Before reciting the names, hang the seven paper strips on a string to wear as a cap, and put it on your head before you begin the prayers. And you should have sealing wax with you. When the jinn appear, take one of the written paper strips and recite the text to them, and say: *Which of you is the owner of this strip and the owner of this patch?*[44]

One of them will reply: 'I am its owner.' Ask him: *What is your name?* He will reply: 'I am so-and-so.' Write his name at the top of the strip, then say: *Give me your seal!* And take the string with the paper and the wax and seal it at the bottom of the strip as you would seal a written document. Afterwards speak in the same way to each of them until you finish with the seventh.

Then say: *I conjure you by the names that are on this strip to come and answer to my call when I invoke you!*

Then say: *Be gone. May the blessings of Allah be upon you!*

Thereafter keep the sealed paper strips in a clean place until your need arises, to eat, to drink, to know something, to discover a treasure or buried goods, or anything else. When you call the jinn, they will respond faster than lightning and the flying wind by the permission of the Almighty Allah.

Beware, O brother, do not perform this if you are not strong of

44 The 'patch' is another word for the paper strip.

heart and firm in intention: you should have a stable mind and steady heart, and be versed in retreats and spiritual exercises. If you are not like this, be careful, for if you summon the jinn you will harm yourself. And beware of their gaze, for it reveals what lies concealed in the heart.

WORKING AND MARRIAGE WITH MĀLIKA AL-JAMĀL[45]

This queen rules over seven hundred kings, and each king rules over seven hundred jinn tribes, and none knows each tribe's number except God Almighty. If you want to marry this queen, go into seclusion for a period of twelve days, starting from a Sunday, and be in a clean state of body, dress and place. Burn the incense all night and after each obligatory prayer while reciting the conjuration. The incense is benzoin, aloeswood, styrax, frankincense and gum mastic.

The conjuration should be recited one hundred times after each obligatory prayer and one thousand times at midnight with the incense burning during the twelve days of seclusion. Each night write the talismans on the palms of your hands, then put your right palm under the left over your chest while going to sleep. On the eighth night you will be awakened, and you will see many women like the moon, who will say to you: 'Take one of us and leave your work.' Reply to them: *I do not wish for any but Mālika Al-Jamāl*, and they will leave you. On the twelfth night, women like the moon will come to you and between them will stand Mālika Al-Jamāl like the sun, wearing a dress and ornaments with unseen beauty,[46] and behind them will be a judge. They will greet you with peace. Reply to them with the greeting of peace too. A marriage license will be arranged for you to gain the hand of Mālika Al-Jamāl.

Praise God for this conjuration:

45 The Queen of Beauty.

46 This means that such beauty is previously unseen: it is beyond praise and comparison.

Manqariush, Manqariush, 'Aantartush, 'Aantartush, A'anitush, A'anitush, Harhaztakh, Harhaztakh, Ashmakhshakh, Ashmakhshakh, Mashlamal, Mashlamal, 'Artaghun, 'Artaghun, Samrashun, Samrashun, Hamaltas'ashthamiyal, Hamaltas'ashthamyal. Answer me and come to me, O Malika Al-Jamal, to accomplish our undiminished marriage: it will be enchantment and dependence on God. Hurry! Quickly! At once!

This is the talisman that should be written on the right palm:

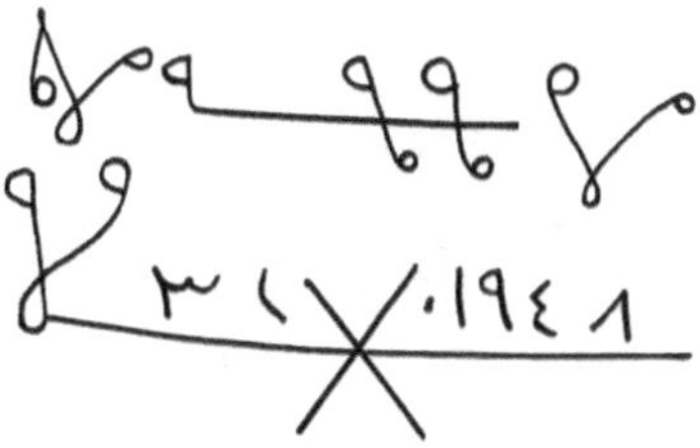

This is the talisman that should be written on the left palm:

ADJURATION OF SARŪKH

If you want to perform this operation, draw this talismanic figure on paper:

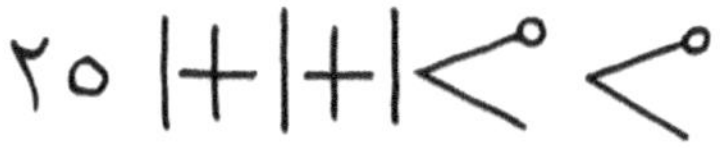

This is the summoning, the name of the king, and the name of the aide. This is the adjuration:

Tarīkh, Tarīkh, Biṭaṭīsh, Biṭaṭīsh, Sām, Sām, Harūsh, Harūsh, come, O Sarūkh, son of the Great Iblīs, by the right of the lord of the length and the width, and the spirit of the idols and fire worshippers, and in the name of haste, Maṭaṭ, Maṭaṭ, come, O Sarūkh, Sama'iā, Maṭa'iā. Now! Quickly! Immediately!

Recite this adjuration two hundred and six times.

This is the talismanic figure:

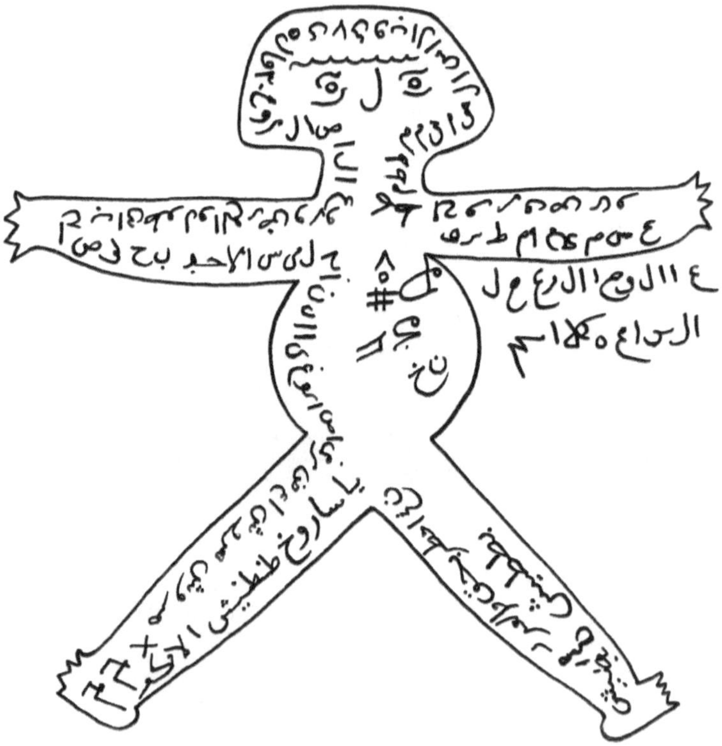

To dismiss the jinnī, burn the paper in the brazier with an incense of frankincense and gum benzoin.

TO BRING ʿAAYNA, THE DAUGHTER OF AL-AḤMAR

It is proven. She will serve you for everything you want. Fast for seven days, eating no animals or any product derived from them, and on the seventh night make a figure of a woman from wax and write these names upon it:

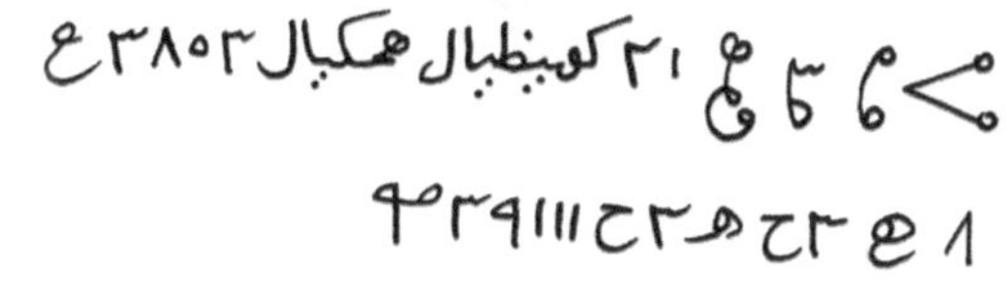

Then burn the incense from gum benzoin and recite the conjuration seventy times. She will come to you. Make a pact with her for everything you want. If you desire to marry her, tell her: *You are of Fire, I am of Earth*, and command her to cool her body. Marry her on condition that you will not have intercourse with another woman, or else you will be harmed.

This is the conjuration:

Baṭārsh, Baṭārsh, Azlī, Azlī, steed lord Bihanṭal, Hanṭal, Saksakas, Majaz, Makhirān, Qawṣān, Qawmān, rider of horsemen, inform me of what this will cost me.

He hath loosed the two seas. They meet.[47] *Answer me, O ʿAayna, O daughter of Al-Aḥmar, and your prince Aba Yaqub Al-Aḥmar with his soldiers. I conjure you Bishanʿaṭāsh, Shamṭāsh, Hayāsh, Hūyāsh, Zarbiāsh, Hūyāsh, Kahliāsh. Hasten, hasten with your presence before the destruction and the lightnings. Now! Quickly! Immediately!*

47 Sūrat ar-Raḥmān: 19.

4

SUMMONING THE PERSONAL QARĪN

TO SUMMON THE QARĪN WITHOUT INCENSE OR FASTING

Sit in a dark place and recite these two names one thousand times:

Ya Qarīb, Ya Mujīb[1]

After that recite the conjuration twenty-one times and you will hear the thin voice of the qarīn speaking to you without seeing his figure. This is the conjuration:

Ṭawmānash, Ṭawmānash, Af'akiūsh, Af'akiūsh, 'Aiūsh, 'Aiūsh, where are the strong armies, where are the 'afārīt of the Fire, the Earth, the Air, and the Water? Answer, O Ahjamliyail, come and listen, O Meṭaṭron, and bring me the qarīna of so-and-so or the qarīn of so-and-so by the right of Barhash, Barhash, Ghālmash, Ghālmash, Qalanhūd, Qalanhūd, Barshān, Barshān.

Lo! it is from Solomon, and lo! it is: In the name of Allah the Beneficent, the Merciful; Exalt not yourselves against me, but come unto me as those who surrender.[2]

Quickly! Willingly! Allah, Lord of the Worlds.[3] *Bring me the qarīna of so-and-so by the right of Faqaj Makhamat, by the benevolence of Haimutha, and by the right of Ahiā, Sharāhiā, Adonai, Aṣbaot, El, Shadai!*

AN EASY WAY TO SUMMON THE QARĪN

Burn incense of *karakhīm*[4] and lotus over a flame and recite: *Ya Qarīb, Ya Mujīb* three hundred and thirteen times and this conjuration seven times:

1 The Near One, the Responder.
2 Sūrat an-Naml: 30–31.
3 Sūrat al-Fātiḥah: 2.
4 I have only encountered this ingredient in this text, and in no other grimoire or Arabic occult manuscript. Though I suspect it is of vegetable origin it is absent from Arabic botanical dictionaries. It might be a local synonym for a plant or perhaps a foreign word.

Barhatiyah, Barhatiyah, Karīr, Karīr, Arqash, Arqash, Barshān, Barshān, come, O Marjān, and you, O Meṭaṭron, and you, O Shūghāl the 'Ifrīt, bring me the qarīn of so-and-so at this hour!

Wheresoever ye may be, Allah will bring you all together. Lo! Allah is able to do all things.[5] *And by the right of Ahiā, Sharāhiā, Adonai, Aṣbaot, El, Shadai, hurry and quickly, O ye noble viziers, and you, O Ṭamriāṭ and O Ḍ'aīq,*[6] *and you, O Hadliākh, bring the qarīna of so-and-so by the right of: In the Name of Allah, the Most Beneficent, the Most Merciful.*

(An 'ifrīt) of the Jinn said: I will bring it thee before thou canst rise from thy place. Lo! I verily am strong and trusty for such work.[7]

Repeat this fifty times.[8]

Hurry, hurry! Quickly, quickly! At once, at once! By the right of Ṭawrash, Ṭawrash, Kamwarash, Kamwarash, Bimahai, Bimsaihaṭal, Arghāsh, bring me the qarīna of so-and-so!

The qarīn will answer you. If you want to dismiss it, recite *Sūrat al-'A'la* or *Sūrat al-Jumu'ah* or the Salute of the Prophet[9] – may Allāh honour him and grant him peace.

5 Sūrat al-Baqarah: 148.
6 In other manuscripts, Ḍ'aīq is given as Sana'aīq, the name of a famous 'ifrīt.
7 Sūrat an-Naml: 39.
8 Although it is not precisely explained in the original text, I think this refers to the Qur'ānic verse An-Naml: 39.
9 This is a short Islamic invocation for greeting the Prophet.

5

THE SEVEN JINN EVICTIONS

THE INVALUABLE SECRET,

and the subjugation of Iblīs's armies

Know that this section contains the greatest secret, the pure yellow gold, the red sulphur, and the blossoming flower. And it contains the submission of each disobedient spirit with the permission of He Whose hand is the governance of all hearts and foreheads. It is the second section of the seven jinn evictions, in which each day of the week has its own eviction.

If a person comes to you on Sunday, whether he is evidently afflicted by a jinnī or in apparently good health,[1] and you want to treat him, write these names on his palm in the Sun's hour on that day, and recite the following over it, and the jinnī will be evicted.

This is what should be written on the palm:

اشواش اشواش اطنجم اطنجم دیایلوا دیایلوا تبوه تبوه فارونده فارونده نشاب نشاب
سنطاري سنطاري اصرعه یا مذهب بحق هذه الاسماء العجل الساعه

Ashuāsh, Ashuāsh, Aṭnajam, Aṭnajam, Daiāyluā, Daiāyluā, Tabuh, Tabuh, Farūndah, Farūndah, Nashāb, Nashāb, Sanṭārī, Sanṭārī, evict him, O Madhab, by the right of these names. Hurry! At once!

This is what should be recited:

Awil, Awil, Hat, Hat, Baqat, Baqat, Baqat, Baqat, Latahin, Latahin, At, At, Jashanash, Jashanash, Tawlah, Tawlah, Althaqari, evict him, O Madhab, by the right of Ghalalaq, Ghalalaq, Bashkalalaq, Bashkalalaq. At once!

1 The person 'evidently afflicted by a jinnī' will show symptoms of possession, the person 'apparently in good health' will also be possessed but will not show visible symptoms of their possession.

EVICTION BY KING ABEYAḌ

For Monday write these names on the palm of the evidently afflicted or apparently healthy person:

صعى صعى كعى كعى ممیال ممیال اصرعه یا ابیض بالذي تجلى للجبل فجعله دكا وخر موسى صعقا

S'ai, S'ai, K'ai, K'ai, Mamyāl, Mamyāl, evict him, O Abeyaḍ, by He who so revealed (His) glory to the mountain He sent it crashing down. And Moses fell down senseless.[2]

Recite these names over him:[3]

Lahash, Lahash, Latish, Latish, Jananbad, Jananbad, Darhash, Darhash, Qanqush, Qanqush, Qarqash, Qarqash, evict him, O Abeyaḍ, by He who so revealed (His) glory to the mountain He sent it crashing down. And Moses fell down senseless.[4]

EVICTION BY KING AḤMAR

For Tuesday write these names on the person's palm in the first hour of the day:

كتب الله لأغلبن أنا ورسلي إن الله قوي عزيز اصرعه يا احمر بطرشل بطرشل طرشل طرشل إن الذين يحادون الله ورسوله أولئك في الأذلين

Allah hath decreed: Lo! I verily shall conquer, I and My messengers. Lo! Allah is Strong, Almighty.[5] *Evict him, O Aḥmar, Biṭarshal, Biṭarshal, Ṭarshal, Ṭarshal. Lo! those who oppose Allah and His messenger, they will be among the lowest.*[6]

2 Sūrat al-A'rāf: 143.
3 I assume the author means over the person's palm, as in the previous rite.
4 Sūrat al-A'rāf: 143.
5 Sūrat al-Mujādilah: 21.
6 Sūrat al-Mujādilah: 20.

Write these letters on his fingers:

س ه ق ي س ه ل ع ط ش ل ف ط ط و ش ل ط ط ى و ش م ى س ا ى ش ل

And recite these names:

Biaykamush, Biaykamush, Tafliush, Tafliush, Harsh, Harsh, Qarsh, Qarsh, Azrash, Azrash, Kaikamush, Kaikamush, Laliush, Laliush, Zatush, Zatush, Karmirash, Karmirash, A'italush, A'italush, Mirkatmah, Mirkatmah. Quickly, O Ahmar, and evict the jinnī from this body by the right of Namuh, Namuh, be not of the sinful. Now! Quickly! Immediately!

EVICTION BY KING BURQĀN

Write these names on the person's palm on Wednesday in the first or the eighth hour:

سبطيح سبطيح احلاكاع احلاكاع اصرعوا هذه الجثة الوحا بحق هذه الاسماء

Sabṭīḥ, Sabṭīḥ, Aḥlākā'a, Aḥlākā'a, evict the jinnī from this body. Hurry, by the right of these names!

And recite these names:

Hath, Hath, Marath, Marath, Taqtaqush, Taqtaqush, Taitaqush, Taitaqush, Haimash, Haimash, Yahahbush, Yahahbush, Hush, Hush, Aliush, Aliush, Marath, Marath. Hurry, O Burqān, and evict the jinnī from this body. Quickly!

EVICTION BY THE JUDGE SHAMHŪRASH

Write these names on the person's palm and recite them as well:

سحلحا سحلحا يس يس يستعجلين يستعجلين بحبلحلا بحبلحلا يطقش يطقش جلجيش جلجيش ارش ارش ديان ديان افعلوا ما تؤمرون الارض به يا شمهورش الوحا العجل الساعة

Saḥlāḥā, Saḥlāḥā, Yas, Yas, Yast'ajālīn, Yast'ajālīn, Baḥablāḥalā, Baḥablāḥalā, Yaṭqash, Yaṭqash, Jāljaish, Jāljaish, Arsh, Arsh, Dayān, Dayān. Do what you are commanded by the earth, O Shamhuresh. Now! Quickly! Immediately!

EVICTION BY KING ZAWBA'AH

Write the names on a piece of paper on Friday and put it under the foot of the evidently afflicted or apparently healthy person, and the jinnī will be evicted:

بشطيخ بشطيخ اخلاط اخلاط اع اع اكا اكا ع ع زرطيل زرطيل اصعقوا به في ظله

Bashṭikh, Bashṭikh, Akhlaṭ, Akhlaṭ, A'a, A'a, Aka, Aka, Ayn, Ayn, Zarṭail, Zarṭail, be stunned in his shadow!

EVICTION BY KING MAYMŪN ABA NUKH

Write these names on the palm of the person afflicted by a jinnī on Saturday in the first hour, and recite them as well, and the jinnī will be evicted:

فيكم فيكم برقشكم برقشكم بككلاح بككلاح ططلبهم ططلبهم وقام بمطيبوخ شلايين
وقامبمطيبوخ شلايين الارض الارض يا ميممون ولقد علمت الجنة انهم لمحضرون

Faikam, Faikam, Barqashkam, Barqashkam, Bakaklāḥ, Bakaklāḥ, Ṭaṭlabham, Ṭaṭlabham, Waqām Bimaṭaibukh Shālaiīn, Waqām Bimaṭaibukh Shālaiīn, Alārdh, Alārdh, O Maymūn, whereas the jinn know well that they will be brought before (Him).[7]

7 Sūrat aṣ-Ṣāffāt: 158.

Bibliography

Al-Rawi, A. K. (2009). The Arabic Ghoul and its Western Transformation. *Folklore* 120 (3), 291–306.

Asar, A. A. (2010). *Peace of Mind: Healing of Broken Lives.* Universal Mercy of America Foundation.

Bearman, P. Bianquis, Th. Bosworth, C. E. E. van Donzel, W. P. (1960). *Encyclopaedia of Islam*, Second Edition. Brill Academic Publishers, Leiden.

Bilu, Y. (1981). Pondering "The Princes of the Oil": New Light on an Old Phenomenon. *Journal of Anthropological Research* 37 (3), 269–278.

Bulkeley, K. Adams, K. Davis, P. M. (2009). *Dreaming in Christianity and Islam: Culture, Conflict, and Creativity.* Rutgers University Press, New Brunswick, New Jersey.

Daiches, S. (1913). *Babylonian oil magic in the Talmud and in later Jewish literature.* Oxford University Press, Oxford.

Dieste, M. J. L. (2013). Health and Ritual in Morocco: Conceptions of the Body and Healing Practices. *Social, Economic and Political Studies of the Middle East* 109.

Doutté, E. (1909). *Magie et religion dans l'Afrique du Nord.* Typ. A. Jourdan.

El-Shamy, H. M. (1988). *Religion Among the Folk in Egypt.* Praeger.

El-Zein, A. (2009). *Islam, Arabs, and Intelligent World of the Jinn.* Contemporary Issues in the Middle East, Syracuse University Press, Syracuse NY.

———(1996). *The Evolution of the Concept of the Jinn from Pre-Islam to Islam.* D. Phil, dissertation, Georgetown University.

Gingrich, A. (1995). Some Remarks on the Connotation of Jinn in North-Western Yemen. *Quaderni di Studi Arabi* 13, *Divination magie pouvoirs au Yémen*, 199–212.

Harari, Y. (2011). Metatron And The Treasure Of Gold: Notes On A Dream Inquiry Text From the Cairo Genizah. *Continuity and Innovation in the Magical Tradition*, Jerusalem Studies in Religion and Culture, 289–320.

Hentschel, K. (1997). *Geister, Magier und Muslime. Dämonenwelt und Geisteraustreibung im Islam.* Diederichs.

Irwin, R. *The Arabian Nights: A Companion.* Tauris Parke Paperbacks, London, 2004.

Jedrej, M. M. and Shaw, R. (1992). *Dreaming, Religion and Society in Africa.* Studies of Religion in Africa, Vol. 7, Brill Academic Publishers, Leiden.

Khaleel, A. M. (2005). *The Jinn and Human Sickness: Remedies in the Light of the Qur'aan and Sunnah.* Darussalam Publishers, Riyadh.

Kruk, R. (2005). Harry Potter in the Gulf: Contemporary Islam and the Occult. *British Journal of Middle Eastern Studies* 32 (1), 47–73.

Lebling, R. and Shah, T. (2011). *Legends of the Fire Spirits: Jinn and Genies from Arabia to Zanzibar.* Counterpoint, Berkeley, California.

Maarouf, M. (2010). *Jinn Eviction as a Discourse of Power.* Islam in Africa Vol. 8, Brill Academic Publishers, Leiden.

McAuliffe, J. D. (2001). *Encyclopaedia of the Qur'ān* (Volume Five: Si–Z). Brill Academic Publishers, Leiden.

Padwick, C. (1924). Notes on the Jinn and the Ghoul in the Peasant Mind of Lower Egypt. *Bulletin of the School of Oriental and African Studies* 3 (03), 421–446.

Rothenberg, C. (2013). *Spirits of Palestine: Gender, Society, and Stories of the Jinn.* Lexington Books, Lanham, Maryland.

Sengers, G. (2003).*Women and Demons: Cultic Healing in Islamic Egypt.* International Studies in Sociology and Social Anthropology, Brill Academic Publishers, Leiden.

Swick, L. J. (2014). *Dreaming: The Sacred Art: Incubating, Navigating and Interpreting Sacred Dreams for Spiritual and Personal Growth.* SkyLight Paths, Woodstock, Vermont.

The Holy Qur'ān, translation by Saheeh International and Yusuf Ali.

Trimingham, J. S. (1965). *Islam in Ethiopia.* Routledge, London.

Tritton, A. S. (1934). Spirits and Demons in Arabia. *Royal Asiatic Society Journal*, 1934, 716–60.

Worrell, W. H. (1916). Ink, Oil and Mirror Gazing Ceremonies in Modern Egypt. *Journal of the American Oriental Society* 36, 37–53.

SELECTED MANUSCRIPTS AND BOOKS IN TRANSLATION

Al-Buni, A. *Magic of the Lights.*

——— *The Book of the Sun of Gnosis and the Subtleties of Elevated Things.*

Al-Iraqi, A. Q. *Moon of the Moons in the Unveiling of Secrets.*

As-Semmoumi, M. Personal notebook. Casablanca.

Al-Sha'er, M. Personal notebook. Egypt.

Al-Tilimsani, Ibn Al-Hajj. *The Book of the Suns of Lights and the Treasures of Secrets.*

Al-Toukhi, A. F. Al-Sayid. (1997). *The Great Magic.* Al-Maktabah Al-Thaqafiah, Beirut.

———(1991). *Magic of Barnukh, the Greatest Secret of the sage Barnukh the Sudanese sorcerer.* Al-Maktabah Al-Thaqafiah, Beirut.

Pseudo-Ibn Al-Hajj Al-Kabir. *Crown of the Kings and Goal of the Owner and the Owned in Pleas of the Kings.*
Pseudo-Ibn Sina. *Book of the wonders of Plato, Treasure of the Mysteries in Conjuring the Jinn and Dismissing the Resident Jinn*, Vol. 2.
Unidentified author. Personal notebook with proven methods. Egypt.
Unidentified author. *The Book of the Qareen*, Mus'haf dhusim.

Index of conjurations

CHAPTER 1
Seeking guidance 2
If you want to see something in your dream 2
To see whatever you wish in a dream 2
For dream revelation by the jinnī Kharbaṭ 5

CHAPTER 2
Mandal of Abba Deebaj 6
Proven mandal 9
Mandal of the seven ways 10
Proven mandal 12
Proven mandal 14
Mandal of the Seven Kings 15
Celestial mandal 16
Proven mandal 17
Proven mandal 19
Scrying by yourself 20
Scrying by yourself 21
Conjuration of King Maymūn 22
The mandal of Nahuil 25

CHAPTER 3
Twelve Workings of the Jinn 29
The first working 29
The second working 30
The third working of Shams Al-Qaramīd, daughter of King Al-Abeyaḍ 30
The fourth working 32
The fifth working 32
The sixth working 33
The seventh working 34
The eighth working 36
The ninth working 36
The tenth working 38
The eleventh working 39
The twelfth working of Aba Yaqub Al-Aḥmar 39
Invocation of the Seven Mayamin 41
The first application 42
The second application 42
The third application 43
The fourth application 43
The fifth application 43
The sixth application 44
The seventh application 44
The eighth application 44
The ninth application 45
The tenth application 45
The eleventh application 46
The twelfth application 46
Summoning a whispering jinnī for reading private thoughts 48
Working of Taresh, the king of the resident jinn 50
The rebuke of King Taresh 51

Proven experiment of a jinnī 51
Employment of a jinnī for attraction, arousal and binding sleep 52
Working of the six daughters 52
Working of Maymūn the Abductor 54
If you want to fraternise with the pious jinn so that they will fulfill your needs and hasten to please you 55
Working and marriage with Mālika Al-Jamāl 58
Adjuration of Sarūkh 59
To bring 'Aayna, the daughter of Al-Aḥmar 61

CHAPTER 4
To summon the qarīn without incense or fasting 63
An easy way to summon the qarīn 63

CHAPTER 5
The invaluable secret, and the subjugation of Iblīs's armies 66
Eviction by King Abeyaḍ 67
Eviction by King Aḥmar 67
Eviction by King Burqān 68
Eviction by the Judge Shamhūrash 68
Eviction by King Zawba'ah 69
Eviction by King Maymūn Aba Nukh 69

www.ingramcontent.com/pod-product-compliance
Lightning Source LLC
Chambersburg PA
CBHW030308100526
44590CB00012B/565